I0210312

A Mouton Coat

A Mouton Coat

The Hunt for a Mother's Story

Full Court Press
Englewood Cliffs, New Jersey

First Edition

Published in the United States of America
by Full Court Press, 601 Palisade Avenue
Englewood Cliffs, NJ 07632
www.fullcourtpressnj.com

Author's Note: Names, identities, and locations of a number of people in this book have been altered in the interest of privacy.

ISBN 978-1-938812-08-8
Library of Congress Control No. 2013932321

Editing and Book Design by Barry Sheinkopf
for Bookshapers (www.bookshapers.com)

Colophon by Liz Sedlack

For Solomon

1

A Mouton Coat

I SAW MY MOTHER FOR the last time in the stifling summer of 1946. This was in the days before air conditioning, when there was no escape from steamy Bronx apartments. In the street, when you played Potsy, a game like Hop Scotch, the soles of your shoes stuck to the sidewalk, and when you picked up the key or whatever you were using for a potsy, your fingers burned. If you were scrunched in the gutter, shooting marbles, they got stuck in the tar and stared up at you like dead fish-eyes. In front of our apartment house, old ladies, seated on wooden folding chairs, fanned themselves with newspapers, infants in carriages screamed for air, and I feared something terrible. Actually, the worst had already happened. A year earlier, my father, haunted by depression, had killed himself. Now there were three remaining occupants of our apartment—my mother, myself, and Grandpa Louis, my mother's father. Louis slithered about, incommunicado as usual, but my mother was silent, too, and that was unusual.

She would sit by the window, wrapped in a pink chenille bathrobe, almost disappearing into the floral armchair print. Her stillness, tinged with desperation, frightened me. Sometimes she sighed with longing for my father; at least I thought it was my father she wanted. With the certainty of a nine-year-old, I knew he was still around someplace, if only we both could find him.

She seemed certain of nothing. I felt I was losing her, as I had years earlier, when she went away for several months to a place for people who were feeling sad.

I was wise to worry. One morning I found her in the kitchen, attired in a mouton fur coat, even though it was hot enough to fry eggs on the sidewalk. That's what they said in New York when the temperature soared, and sometimes the newspapers showed pictures of some clown squatting on the concrete, making an egg sizzle.

Looking at my mother, I thought of the eggs, and I wanted her to cook something, clean out the refrigerator where she kept her diabetes medicine—anything that would keep her with me. I could tell from the suitcase in the front hall that she intended to go away, without any warning, just like the last time.

But I couldn't prevent her departure. Inch by inch, the mouton coat moved toward me, inviting me in, locking me out, as usual. I was my mother's "sometime" daughter—sometimes close, sometimes a burden. If I were better, she wouldn't get sick like this, I thought. If she were better, she'd act like other mothers and not go off to a job, political meetings, or sadness-fixing hospitals. A sudden whiff of perfume filled me with love and longing. I buried my face in the fur and hugged her close. I could feel her body twitching, and I knew she was crying. She said something, but I burrowed deep, so I couldn't hear. Shutting out the sound didn't help the terror. *I'll never see her again,* I thought.

I don't remember how we became dislodged; perhaps other people helped. They must have been there, those people, because my mother went off to the home of her brother, Bernie, and I wound up with my father's parents, Grandpa Philip and Grandma Kate, the Sonkins. They were frequent baby sitters, their apartment a second home. I'd stayed with them the first time my mother disappeared, and they spelled instant safety: Soon after I walked through the door and munched a few pieces of my grandmother's *rugelach,* I decided to block my mother out of my mind.

I acted as if nothing unusual was happening, and so did Kate, Philip, and their unmarried adult children who lived with them, Aunt Sylvia and Uncle Robert. Although I knew they loved me dearly, the Sonkins weren't prone to talking about feelings. Their idea was simply to carry on, which they did with utter devotion.

The summer heat continued and, on the street I played Potsy with another set of friends far into the dusk. Every night, I made sure I was the last one to go inside, so that I'd be too tired to think about my mother before falling asleep. Aunt Sylvia bought me ice cream sodas at Mr. Trott's drug store. I collected movie star postcards, at a penny a pop, from a machine on Mr. Trott's counter. You never knew which movie star you were going to get, James Cagney or Anne Baxter or someone you didn't like very much, like Joan Crawford. I lined up the female stars on my pillow before I went to bed, so anyone of them could substitute for my mother.

Like a koala bear cub, I was looking for a place to attach myself. My aunt presented herself, a sturdy, reliable tree; but I had to be sure. I rummaged through her neat closet, looking for evidence of Sylvia's reality—rayon suits with short skirts and peplum jackets, piles of nylon stockings in ample supply after wartime shortages, tasteful jewelry including several silver pieces she'd made herself. Yes, she certainly seemed to be there, but in the middle of the night, in the room we shared, I'd check it out. "Aunt Sylvia, are you awake?" A murmur as she turns over. I cough until she's startled. "What is it?"

"Nothing."

The darkness made the "nothing" bigger and emptier. I couldn't give the void its proper name because my mother's absence was never discussed. No one ever suggested I might find it disturbing. No one explained why she was gone. I assumed the reason was her sadness problem. But it didn't matter where she was, because I knew she was gone forever.

A month or so after I moved in with my grandparents, someone called to say that my mother was dead. Her diabetes had caused her death, Aunt Sylvia told me. When it got very bad, you went into a deep sleep, and you might not be able to wake up.

I knew my mother suffered from diabetes, which wasn't like a cold or chickenpox. Doctors could fix those diseases, but they could only fix diabetes a little bit, so you had to take care of yourself. My mother injected herself with medicine every day. If she got dizzy, she had to eat an orange right away to avoid passing out. She even kept oranges in her desk at school, where she taught other children like me.

Aunt Sylvia explained that being very sad, as my mother was at this time, could make your diabetes get out of control. Then all the medicines didn't do any good, even if you were in a hospital.

Okay, no surprise. She was gone, and if she didn't have to care about me, I didn't have to care about her. No more of her sorrow, dizzy spells, playing together at the piano, writing stories, walking in the park. Wait a minute—how did the last three sneak in there? I didn't want to think about the things I would miss and the weak-in-the-knees feeling I got from loving her so much. I dwelled on the good-riddances, blew them up to zeppelin-size, and floated them skyward. Then I exploded the ship, my own private *Hindenburg*.

Life went on without her, so there.

I had Aunt Sylvia, so there.

One day Sylvia introduced me to a man she said was a good friend. He'd been overseas during the war, and now she wanted me to get to know him. She didn't say she loved him or anything like that, because of the Sonkin taboo on feelings, particularly good feelings. It was okay to be worried or hurt—in fact, feeling hurt was the norm—but happiness was unreliable, sad events far more certain.

The man bought tickets for a baseball game at Yankee Stadium, just a few blocks from my grandparents' apartment. On a fall day, we walked through Joyce Kilmer Park, ablaze with turning leaves, and I observed that he resembled my favorite movie star, Gene Kelly.

At the Stadium, we munched hot dogs while sunlight flickered across the field. Joe DiMaggio, for all his graceful gait and bottomless stamina, was in a slump. He struck out twice, and the crowd booed. The man and I looked at each other, horrified at such sacrilege, as if they were trampling a saint's statue. To soothe our distress, we swilled down a round of soda pop, and then another. We belched and smiled at one another; he won my heart.

A few months later, the man became my Uncle Leo at a home wedding I thought the grandest thing ever. We had recently purchased a console that played phonograph records automatically, one after the other, like a jukebox, right in your own home. I was in charge of the music, and I played "The Girl that I Marry" over and over, because that was Leo's favorite song. In between, I passed *hors d'oeuvres*, marvelously tiny, and thought how great it was to feel happy.

Aunt Sylvia wore a pink suit with a full below-the-calf skirt, the "New Look," and a broad-brimmed hat with a gold veil. Suddenly, I remembered my mother telling me that her own wedding outfit had been apple green. Was it a gown or a suit like Sylvia's? I wondered, and who had been at the wedding? A lump rose in my throat, surprising me so much that I almost scratched a brand-new record. I regained control. *Who cares what she wore? The only thing that matters is what's happening here, now.*

Here and now continued. Sylvia and Leo moved into their own apartment, fortunate to find one in the post-war shortage. They decorated it just so—floral print sofa and matching love seat, forest green carpeting, walk-in closets with plenty of room for extra shelves because Sylvia had to arrange things neatly.

A few years later, Grandma Kate died, Robert got his own apartment, and Grandpa Philip and I moved in with Leo and Sylvia, who were expecting a child. It was goodbye to *House and Garden*, hello to chaotic closets. I was grateful to Leo for accepting an assortment of relatives with such equanimity. Quarters were cramped, tempers sometimes flared, but no one thought of any arrangement other than being together. With all its quirks, my family's devotion was a fortress. "My son-in-law is the Rock of Gibraltar," Grandpa Philip used to say. The rock kept me safe; but the trade-off was to suppress thoughts of my mother. She had failed me; the Sonkins proved that they would be there. I had only one family.

Years later, when I was happily married and pregnant with my first child, I had a mantra—"be there, be there, be there." My children, I swore, would have a mother and a father, too, because my husband, Solomon, was life-affirming and well balanced. I loved him for those qualities. He wouldn't be killing himself any time soon.

I devoted myself to full-time motherhood, pretty easy to do, because it was the norm. By the time I went back to work, my three children were trusting people, on firm ground, a great achievement in my book. They didn't inhabit a world where rotten things could be expected.

But it's only natural for those things to catch up with you sometimes. One day, while at a crowded outdoor concert, someone pushed my hand against my breast and I felt something hard.

The I-found-a-lump story has been written hundreds of times. Is it there, or isn't it? Can you feel it, too, dearly beloved husband? Maybe if I don't touch it, it will go away. It's still there; I guess I should call the doctor. He says, It's probably nothing, but let's have a mammogram. There's a shadow on the mammogram. He says, It's probably a cyst, but let's have a biopsy. Oops—end of the line: Let's have a mastectomy.

I was recovering from surgery, figuring my chances of still "being there" for my children, when an intern popped in with a questionnaire. No, I told him, there was no family history of breast cancer. I knew most of the Sonkins well, even distant cousins, and none of them had had cancer of any sort. It never occurred to me that there was another side to my genetic heritage; that's how deeply I had buried my mother.

Somehow I lucked out with this breast-cancer business. The years went by—five, ten—then past the time when they stop counting survival rates—fifteen, almost eighteen—and I was still "being there." Breast cancer got integrated into my life, a part of being me. I never speculated about why the cancer landed at my door. Some women get that kind of special delivery, that's all—or is it a bomb, timed to go off?

In the 1990s, scientists discovered two mutated genes in Ashkenazi Jewish women related to premenopausal breast cancer. BRCA1 and BRCA2, the so-called "breast cancer" genes, are among the most important genes ever discovered, and the most worrisome. If you've got either one, your chances of developing breast cancer are somewhere between 85 and 90 percent. I read that a medical task force recommended early mammograms, starting at age twenty-five, for women with either of the genes, and for their daughters.

I clipped the article, not comprehending why. After all, there was no cancer in my family, and only three percent of breast cancers are gene-related. But the article seemed to be pointing a bony finger straight at me—that prototypical Ashkenazi Jewish woman with premenopausal breast cancer. I, with an Ashkenazi Jewish woman daughter just twenty-nine years old, brimming with life, suddenly under the shadow of her loving mother's DNA, a daughter who, perhaps, should be having a mammogram now, this very minute. Impossible. We couldn't have the gene, but all the time, I knew we could, because I had lopped off one whole side of my family.

For the first time in decades, I thought about my Grandma Minnie, my mother's mother. When I was a small child living with my parents, Minnie, and her husband Louis, lived across the hall. To reach their apartment, I had to traverse an expanse of black and white tiles, like walking to the end of the ocean, because I didn't want to reach my destination. I would pull on my mother's hand, fearful of what awaited us behind the brown steel door with chipped numbers.

Darkness. The furniture was mahogany, a sharp contrast to the stainless steel that adorned our own art deco living room. The room was dark, curtains drawn, just a sliver of light across the linoleum floor. A dank odor prevailed, a mixture of cooking oil and medications.

Sometimes Minnie was in the kitchen; more frequently, she was dozing on the bed, black oxfords on, ready to get up and resume her chores when she could. She always smiled when she saw me, but I thought it odd that she didn't play with me, take me to the park, or tell stories as my other grandmother did. She was already a ghost, and I associated her with a sorrow that seemed to be catching, because my mother was often sad.

When I was three, I went somewhere in a car because Minnie had died—not to the funeral, most likely to the Sonkins, who always stood by, ready to take over.

Why had I never given serious thought to Minnie? My

mother loved her dearly, I know. I have some old photographs of the pair—my mother, a fresh-faced teenage girl with bangs; Minnie, a handsome matron, prematurely gray hair pulled tight in a bun. My mother wore knickers, an argyle sweater, and a wide smile. Almost always they were hand in hand, arm in arm, shoulder to shoulder. In one photo, my mother was jumping up and down behind Minnie, dancing a little dance.

Shortly before I was born, my mother sculpted a handsome bust of Minnie that stood on the bookcase/desk in our living room. If you opened the desk, you had to first remove the bust, so that it didn't get broken. We took care with Minnie.

After I read about the genes, I asked Aunt Sylvia how Minnie had died. "I'm pretty sure it wasn't breast cancer," Sylvia said. "She complained that her stomach hurt."

Good God, I thought, has Sylvia forgotten that breast cancer can metastasize? That's when you die, and in the old days, you only talked about it at the end, because the pain was so bad you couldn't hide anymore.

I couldn't hide anymore, either. I needed to know about Minnie.

To obtain a death certificate from the City of New York, you have to say why you want it. I wrote "genetic research," as if my grandmother, Minnie Paley, was a scientific project. I couldn't imagine how human Minnie would soon become.

The signature on the certificate belonged to our family physician, a good friend in the days when doctors made house calls. He was a tall, dignified man, so patient he even put up with me, a panicky child who kicked doctors in the groin. He must also have visited Minnie in that gloomy mahogany bedroom across the hall.

Most often, a death certificate contains only a few explanatory words, "cancer" or "coronary disease." This doctor left an entire case history: *Carcinoma of the breast, October 1929. Carcinoma of the rectum, March 1937. Metastases to liver, lungs, January 1940.* I felt he was sending a message to posterity, and that would be me. He had taken Minnie's hand, the one that lay exhausted, inert, on her wrinkled sheet—and put it into mine.

I experienced a mood of séance, a filmy vision of the past. I could see our doctor sitting upright in Minnie's soda chair, scribbling notes on the kitchen table. He rummages through his black bag, making sure he's replaced the vial of pain medication he has just shot into his patient. He flips through the evening newspaper, then returns to the bedroom to see if Minnie has quieted down. Her eyes are tight shut, her breathing is shallow. He takes her blood pressure again. Little time left, little time before he'll be writing it down for the City of New York and that annoying child across the hall.

Thank you doctor, from the royal brat. You revived Minnie for me, made us cancer sisters—more years of survival for me, but in our stars, no doubt, the same screwed-up chromosome.

I'd been luckier, but was it luck? I remembered that Grandpa Louis, Minnie's husband, was a terrible miser, wrangling over every purchase he was forced to make. Although he consulted doctors, he fiercely resisted paying their bills. Louis was truly deranged on the subject of money, and with an expensive illness, he would have been at his most horrible.

So when Minnie discovered the lump, what had happened?

Some women see a doctor right away, others hang on to the delusion that "it can't really be there." If you have a miser husband, there's good reason to stick with denial. But, finally, you have to confide in someone, a daughter most likely, who takes the father to task—"I'm calling the doctor tomorrow, Pop." Or maybe the daughter calls secretly. By the time the doctor writes a medical notation—*Carcinoma of the breast, October 1929*— the cancer could be pretty advanced.

The daughter, my mother, was twenty-three years old in 1929. She must have been terrified by her mother's diagnosis, fearful for the next eleven years, waiting for the shoe to drop. Minnie's cancer spread to her colon just three months after I was born in 1937, leaving my mother to care for a desperately ill mother as well as an infant. I could understand her sadness in Minnie's apartment, straightening up the medicine bottles, sweeping the kitchen, opening the window to let in some air. I could understand why she had sculpted a memorial bust.

With this first lifting of the shadows, I wanted to know more. Until I read Minnie's death certificate, my mother was a woman who hadn't been there for me, even though it wasn't her fault, so I was better off not thinking about her. But now I regretted the great chasm between us. I knew just as much about my birth mother as an adoptee. Clara Paley Sonkin wasn't simply dead—she'd "gone missing," as the British say, carried off by circumstances and my own determination to forget. My father's family was quite content to have her missing. My mother's family was quite content to have *me* missing. After she died, I never saw them again.

I was furious at them all, the dear ones who cared for me the deserters who cared not a whit. What kind of child rearing is that, letting a memory expire from lack of oxygen? The vision of a departed mother needs to be tended: "Your mother was a beautiful bride in an apple green gown," "Your mother became a teacher because she loved small children," "I remember that, once, your mother brought a basket of roses to the Passover Seder," "Your mother met your father at a party, a movie, a cousin's house"—take your pick, but bring her to life. A good word would have been best, but any word would have done.

Well, now I had some word. Diabetes wasn't the only illness stalking my mother; there had been another killer waiting in the wings. It had slain Minnie, it had chopped off my breast, and it could be taking aim at my lovely daughter.

I went to a medical center and got tested for the breast cancer gene.

"Are you sure you want to know?" asked my husband Solomon before we set off. He was supportive but uncertain about opening doors that might have tigers behind them. I left him in the waiting room, glancing at a magazine, chatting with the receptionist in his amiable fashion, but I knew he wasn't happy. He didn't really want to learn whether a wayward gene might be threatening our good fortune. Solomon is an optimist, and it helps to stay positive if you don't look for trouble.

He didn't know how strongly the gene and my mother were linked in my mind. The gene was a sentinel calling her back to me, along with Minnie and all of the Ashkenazi Jewish female relatives who had preceded us.

We were linked, starting with the mutation's source, that first gene Mama. I could see her, rosy-cheeked and full-breasted, working the wheat fields somewhere in the

Ukraine, hawking eggs in a marketplace in Belarus, or chopping gefilte fish in Lodz. It's a bright summer day, and as she goes about her business, a cell goes crazy on a chromosome. That morning, Mama's DNA was cool, but by nightfall, it's raced out of control, become possessed by a *dybbuk*—a tortured spirit that enters the bodies of the living. This genetic monster is barely a wisp of matter, invisible to the human eye, but it passes death along. As women die of breast cancer, Mama's descendants are perplexed. Sin is blamed, fate, and also "the evil eye." The gene women pray, don amulets, practice whatever magic they know, even the magic of the mammogram, but the deaths continue, down to the present day.

A few weeks after the blood test, I learned that I, too, was possessed by the *dybbuk*; I had BRCA 2.

Solomon and I sat in the genetic counselor's office, not cheered by the bouquet of daisies on her desk. We jotted down statistics, discussed whether my children might want to be tested, and then there was a long pause.

Finally, the counselor asked what I knew about the medical history of my mother's family. Researchers need complete family histories to further scientific knowledge. In some families, just about every woman with the gene gets breast cancer; in others, only some women do. Why this happens is a major puzzle, the counselor said.

Clearly, she was hoping I had something to contribute.

I recalled a first cousin my age, Janet, the daughter of my mother's brother, Bernie Paley. And I remembered two older female cousins, Anna and Emily, sisters, to whom my mother was pretty close. Were they Paleys also? I hadn't seen any of these women in more than five decades.

I didn't know their married names and, in the case of the older cousins, even their maiden name. "I don't think I could find them," I told the counselor. "Sorry."

In the next few weeks, my mother appeared in my dreams for the first time since childhood. In one dream, she was wearing her mouton coat and carrying a suitcase, as if returning from a journey. I took the suitcase, and her hand crumbled, like a piece of old newspaper. Opening the suitcase, I discovered only darkness. Whose insides was I probing? Hers? Mine? They seemed to be the same.

Now that my mother was back, she didn't want to go away. There she was, night after night, with the apparent object of having me find her.

To do that, I'd have to start the painful process of remembering, and I'd have to locate those long-gone, didn't-care-for-you-much cousins. It promised to be a soul-searing search, but at the end, my mother would be there, restored to me in some fashion. I'd be able to see her whole, from an adult's point of view. I rationalized that ferreting out her family was no more than my duty. I owed it to science, to my daughter, to add one case history more to the reams of data.

The place to begin was with my own vague memories. To jog my mind, I gathered the few objects I had that belonged to her—copper portraits she had crafted, of an idealized African warrior and his mate, her favorite reproduction of a Van Gogh painting, and an afghan of many colors she'd knitted at the end of World War II.

I remembered her working on the afghan, a jumble of wool at her feet, picking through the scraps carefully so that each square would be a different color or pattern. This rich kaleidoscope wasn't destined for servicemen, since the war had just ended. It was our very own "coat of many colors," and it seemed to signify a new era—for us and the world.

My mother was an excellent craftswoman—she sewed, knitted, crocheted, sculpted, made pottery—and there's not a stitch amiss in the afghan. I assisted with the final stages, spreading out the squares, helping to decide where to place them, and watching as she masterfully stitched together the pieces with heavy black wool.

The black wool is frayed now, joining the squares only tenuously. But I've never had the afghan repaired because I don't want any other stitches but hers. And, miraculously, despite my grandsons' roughhousing, the afghan has never come apart.

Early one morning, before Solomon was awake, I went downstairs, turned on the television set, and wrapped myself in the afghan. I thought of Jean Cocteau's classic movie *Orpheus*, in which messages from the underworld are received through the radio. I wished my TV could be such a transmitter, so the job ahead wouldn't be so difficult. I wanted my mother to tell me her story, or at least serve as my own personal fact checker.

I didn't realize then that the facts could never be checked. I would have to conjure, invent, and resurrect her. I would have to search for her in the places she might have been and within the context of the year she died—1946. I couldn't imagine how difficult this putting together would be, and that the work would have to be done by the child I once was. I only knew that I was a half-century late, and that I didn't care to be parted from my mother any longer. While alive, she was so often missing from my life, but "it wasn't anybody's fault." That was what I'd always been told. Well, fault or not, she'd hidden from me long enough.

Come out, come out, wherever you are, cries the child within. And the search begins.

2

A Podonoff Greeting

ALONG WITH THE CAUSE of death, Minnie's death certificate told me several things I never knew before. Her parents' names were Sholem and Sarah Podonoff. I had clearly been named for Sarah, since my full name is Sara Jean, and it's the custom of Ashkenazi Jews to name for a beloved dead person.

So right away, I had strong ties to these newly discovered Podonoffs. And the name delighted me—solid, emphatic, ethnic, the perfect place to begin my search.

I guessed that the Podonoff family had come from the city of Minsk in what is present-day Belarus. An obvious assumption; as a child, all of the older people I knew, the Sonkins, the Paleys, came from Minsk. It was because of Minsk that they had a funny accent, and sometimes they even spoke another language, Yiddish, linked to that far-away place.

For me, Minsk was magical, a fearsome fantasy out of the Arabian nights, because bad things happened there. In Minsk, my family had been imprisoned in a bottle, but they'd never say how they had escaped. In fact, they wouldn't talk about Minsk at all. Once, though, I pestered a few words out of an elderly Sonkin aunt. "There were pigs in the streets," she sighed. "*Now* are you satisfied?" My grandparents had figured that the less I knew about Minsk, the safer I was.

Yet Minsk continued to define their world. Grandpa Philip was the president of a huge *landsmanshaften* organization—a lodge made up of people from the same town or district—called the Minsker Independent Benevolent Association, or MIBA. Feeling lost in America, immigrants counted on old country neighbors for socializing. A *landsmanshaft* was the place to find news of the old country, a place to stay, a helping hand—even a mate.

They were an incestuous bunch, these Minskers. It was undoubtedly through the MIBA that Philip Sonkin met Kate Feins and ultimately married her. It was probably through the MIBA that Louis Paley met Minnie Podonoff.

Now I, too, want to meet the Podonoffs.

In the 1900 federal census, which I examine on microfilm at a Mormon Family History Center, I sail through a sea of "P" names, the children of Ellis Island, each one somebody's ancestor, waiting to be claimed.

What, I wonder, was the fate of Carmen Pettinato, age 22, and his boarder, Frank Orestino, 19. Did they make it in America or return to Italy? And what about Stanislaus Podemski, age 28, and wife Frances? So young, so hopeful, I trust all went well for them.

And Carmela Padula, age 50, living on Oliver Street with her mother-in-law, Pasquala. Did Mr. Padula die or never return from going out for the proverbial pack of cigarettes? Somehow I see the pair as abandoned, clinging to one another in the New World like Ruth and Naomi—Carmela and Pasquala, whither thou goest.

The Poddowitz family flits by—Jacob, Sarah, and their children—Lina, Charles, Hyman, Lewis, and Henry—all in a tiny apartment on Water Street. Good luck Poddowitzes. With hard work, you'll get out of there. The Bronx beckons, and then, for your grandchildren, the suburbs, and even California, Florida, the Midwest, or any place else they chose to go. In 1900, your lives may seem constricted, but that's misleading. Actually, you're eagles poised for flight.

My arm grows weary from turning the film; my eyes ache from deciphering long-ago scrawls. The Podonoffs seem to be playing hide and seek, just like my mother. If only I could reach into the machine and pluck them out.

And then, in writing that's barely legible, there they are: Sholem Podonoff, age 45, a peddler, and his wife, Sarah, age 42, both born in Russia. Also in the household are a 19-year-old daughter, Minnie—my Minnie, a cigar maker, and a 13-year-old-son, Abraham. Could he be the father of my mother's two female cousins, Anna and Emily?

The Podonoffs live at 72 Monroe Street on the Lower East Side, an area frequently described as "teeming."

In 1900, Monroe Street was home to nine hundred people. It must have looked a lot like the famous photograph of Hester Street that appears in so many books on New York City—sidewalk stalls lined with goods, horse-drawn carts making deliveries, old men with yarmulkes, young men with straw hats, housewives exchanging gossip, young girls arm in arm, oblivious to the litter around them. One of those girls could have been Minnie, or my mother—or me.

Because I belong here, amid the tumult, in this strange atmosphere of half-light and half-hope. Because this is where my mother is first to be found, in Minnie's vanished world, the matrix that fashioned my mother and all the other first-generation Minsker children. Here, on the Lower East Side, I need to interview the Podonoffs.

I imagine that it's a spring day in 1900, and I'm a woman from the neighborhood making my way through the maze of streets. Under my arm, I carry a pile of census sheets, instructions, and my government identification. I shield these papers against the mud splashed by horse-drawn carts.

Number 72 Monroe Street is a "dumbbell" tenement, so-called because of its shape, a stairway running through the center, four apartments on each landing, two toilets to a floor. Only the rooms in the front or the rear receive direct light. The middle rooms, generally the bedrooms, have to borrow what light they can from dark hallways, the air shafts, and the rear rooms.

Entering Number 72, I'm assaulted by a mass of odors—Jewish cooking, Italian cooking, dank linoleum, musty walls, human waste—welcome and warning intermingled. The air hangs heavy, as if waiting for a weather pattern to shift, but the clouds are perennial. I almost trip over two little girls playing jacks in the hall, the game illuminated by a sliver of light from an open door.

Three women push past, castigating the girls for being in the way, eying me with suspicion. In this building, where everyone knows everyone's business, a stranger merits examination. The papers under my arm reveal my census mission. The government sends people to ask nosy questions, and only God knows what they do with the information. Where these tenants come from, the government is to be avoided. "God bless the Czar and keep him—far away from us," says a character in a Sholem Aleichem story. The tenants can't guess their answers will constitute a legacy, that their posterity will seek them out. They can't imagine they will be loved.

I proceed up the stairs, gingerly passing the jacks players. At the end of the hall, I knock on a heavy metal door.

The door is opened by a young woman with clear blue eyes, an aquiline nose, and thick blonde hair pulled up in a bun. She has high cheek bones and a smooth complexion. She's wearing a shirtwaist with long sleeves and a slim skirt in the Gibson Girl style, the fashion suiting her tall frame.

She invites me into the tiny kitchen, the center of every Jewish household on the Lower East Side. At the stove, a middle-aged woman is stirring a pot of soup. A bare light bulb hangs from the ceiling; newspapers cover the freshly scrubbed floor. There's a square wooden table in the center of the room where an adolescent boy, dressed in knickers and a white shirt, is scribbling his homework.

In Yiddish, the older woman explains that her husband isn't home. She tells me that *mein tukhter, Minnie,* will answer my questions.

I sit down and stare, overjoyed but oppressed by the crumbling brown paint on the walls, the narrowness of the apartment, the obvious inadequacy of Sholem's peddling income. I understand that the family depends on Minnie's work as a cigar maker, and that the future rests on Minnie's making the right marital decisions. To provide for their security, she will marry Louis Paley, a cold, money-driven man, a small manufacturer, a "boss" with the promise of wealth.

Right now, as I copy down Minnie's answers to the government's questions, my mother, one of Minnie's vast supply of eggs, is influenced by these decisions. She will be heir to the family's immigrant insecurities, competitiveness, money battles, quest to succeed—all melded together and absolutely fixed, like the odor in the entry hall. Pulling this legacy apart, deciding when to rebel and when to accept, that will be Clara's task. My terribly modern mother begins here, where Sholem and Sarah speak no English, where the echoes of Minsk still dominate, on a May morning as the century turns.

Wow—who could have guessed that reading the census would prove so informative?

I rewind the microfilm and leave the Mormon Family History Center, the taste of Podonoff still in my mouth.

The next step is to find out where Sholem and Sarah are buried, so that I can learn their death dates and send for their death certificates, important sources of information.

In Brooklyn and Queens, stretched out in rows, are the cemeteries where the immigrant Jews buried their dead. Today, these neighborhoods—Cypress Hills, Glendale, Maspeth, Ridgewood—have become part of the urban sprawl, but in the early 1900s, when the Minsker Independent Benevolent Association and hundreds of other *landsmanshaften* purchased parcels of graves, the cemeteries were "in the country." Visiting was a full-day affair, entailing a carriage ride and lunch in a nearby restaurant.

For most immigrants, these resting places were the first real estate they had ever owned, terribly important. The *landsmanshaften* competed, marking their sections with gates, often of bronze or gold, on which important members "subscribed" their names for a price. Today, many gates have been stolen by drug addicts willing to sell anything for a fix; other gates are in disrepair—plaques tarnished, hinges broken, in mourning for themselves as well as their dead.

Behind which of these desolate gateways do the Podonoffs lie?

I phone every Jewish cemetery, beginning with the biblically inspired—Machpelah, Mt. Carmel, Mt. Hebron, Mt. Hope, Mt. Judah, Mt. Lebanon, Mt. Neboh, Mt. Zion. Then I move on to cemeteries named for great men, Maimonides, Montefiore, and Washington (even though he was not a Jew).

Always, I ask the same question: "I believe my great-grandparents, Sholem and Sarah Podonoff, are buried in your cemetery. Can you tell me when they died?" Always, I get the same reply: "Sorry, they're not here." It sounds as if Sholem and Sarah have stepped out for a moment, visiting Monroe Street perhaps, and will soon return.

My husband Solomon and I have just returned from a London trip, where we visited a historic synagogue endowed by the great philanthropist Sir Moses Montefiore. There was an elaborately carved chair—a throne-like affair—once reserved for Montefiore and now held in readiness for his descendants. The chair, with its lion's-claw feet, impressed me and, as I review the cemeteries I've called, the name Montefiore sticks in my brain, a mystical connection of sorts.

I call Montefiore Cemetery and ask the receptionist to search again. After a wait that seems interminable, she locates Sholem and Sarah. "Sorry," she apologizes, "they were in the old book." Also in the "old book," their son Abraham, whom I'd met in the census as a thirteen-year-old bar mitzvah boy, and Abraham's wife Rachel. The receptionist tells me that Sholem, Sarah, Abraham, and Rachel are buried in the section of a small Minsker organization. I send for death certificates and learn that both Sholem and Abraham died of cancer, Abraham at the youthful age of thirty-nine. These deaths could be evidence of the BRCA2, since the gene is thought to affect males as well as females.

Sholem's death certificate lists Minnie Paley as the person who provided information, but on Sarah's, the informant's first name is illegible; the surname seems to be *Mininkop* or something like that.

The name is tantalizingly familiar but off-kilter; I arrange the letters every which way, drifting to sleep one night in a miasma of vowels and consonants.

Strange dreams emerge—a heavy, full-breasted woman, racing about, shouting, trying to kiss me. She has a round face with a mole on her chin and a single hair growing out of it, black and wiry. Being kissed by her is like colliding with a Brillo pad. As the dream ends, I push her away and sit bolt upright in bed, remembering her name.

Mollie Minkin. She was an aunt of my mother's, obviously another Podonoff sibling, and her visits were manic, memorable for their intensity. How could my brain cells have eased her out so totally? The hairy mole has got to be one answer. I have a feeling Mollie deserved to be forgotten, but it would certainly be helpful to find her now.

The next day, I call Montefiore again and learn that Mollie doesn't rest among the Podonoffs. She isn't even in the "old book."

A thought occurs to me. "Who pays for the upkeep on the Podonoff graves?"

Abraham and Rachel are "maintained," says the receptionist, by a certain Emily Watol.

The minute she says "Emily," five decades worth of cobwebs parted. It's the early 1940s, the war years, and I can see the cousins clearly, Anna and Emily, two young women, hair in pompadours like the Andrews Sisters, oval faces, sharp features, blazing blue eyes—Minnie's eyes and my mother's. Emily wears a uniform—blue and white, a snappy skirt, jaunty hat like a sailor's, and shiny oxfords.

She's in the war, a WAVE or a SPAR, the women's branches of the navy and the Marine Corps. I remember how proud I was to have a cousin in uniform and how disappointed when my mother explained that women didn't actually fight.

Playing "war" with the kids on the street, I longed to be a soldier, not a nurse, the assignment usually given to girls. "I can shoot," I'd yell, pointing a toy gun. My goal was to be like Ike, directing the whole operation, and second best was knowing that a cousin was in the service, helping Ike in some way.

Once in a while, when Emily came home on leave, my mother and I would visit Forest Hills, in Queens, where the sisters lived on a tree-lined street with neat brick houses. Though the house wasn't white like the one in my Dick-and-Jane reader, I thought it quite excellent; there were few other relatives who lived in a house.

In front, there was a special tree. Anna and Emily told me how fairies sprinkled the tree with special dust so it could grow gifts for children who were clever enough to find them. I'd poke around in the dirt and, sure enough, there'd be tiny plastic dolls and trucks about the size of the trinkets that came in the Cracker Jacks box.

Wouldn't it be wonderful to have a tree like in front of my apartment house? I certainly wouldn't mind sharing with the other kids; fairy trees didn't run out of gifts.

The Forest Hills house had another great attribute, a staircase. You could be on one floor and then on the other simply by marching up and down. On the landing, there was a mirror where you could observe yourself coming and going, an excellent reason to come and go as much as possible.

I enjoyed being in that house. I enjoyed my mother's relatives, but just as my mother didn't come along when my father and I visited the Sonkins every Saturday, my father never came to Forest Hills. I didn't think it was natural for the two families to be separated, but everyone else acted as if it were. After my mother's death, when I went to live with the Sonkins, the chasm widened so much that the Podonoffs fell in and dropped out of sight.

Anna and Emily were among the last people to see my mother alive. After she left me in the kitchen of our apartment in the summer of 1946, wearing a mouton coat, my mother went to stay for a few weeks with her brother, Bernie, and his wife, Theresa. She also stayed, for a time, with the two sisters. At least, this is what Aunt Sylvia remembers.

My mother died in West Hill Sanitarium, a mental institution in Riverdale, New York. She was admitted five days before her death on August 23, 1946. According to her death certificate, the admitting problem, and the cause of death, were diabetic complications.

For many years, when I thought about my mother at all, I wondered why she'd been sent to a mental institution for diabetes. If diabetes, not depression, was the problem, why not choose a full-scale hospital? And how had my mother managed to develop diabetic complications when she was so careful about her disease?

On the top shelf of the refrigerator, she kept a hypodermic needle and a small, cold bottle not to be touched by me. The bottle, my mother told me, contained insulin, a substance she needed to stay healthy. She had to stick the needle into the top of the bottle to get the fluid out and then stick the needle into her body. I never saw her doing this injecting business, but I thought it was odd and brave.

My mother carried an orange at all times. If she started to feel faint, a bite of orange could fix things up fast. If she was planning to play tennis, she adjusted the insulin dose, which was what you had to do to prevent trouble.

Remembering how strict my mother was, I'd asked doctor friends over the years how she could have gotten into so much trouble. Vague answers: "Well, they didn't know much about managing insulin in those days," or "Somehow her blood sugar got out of whack." I concluded that my friends were undoubtedly correct. Insulin had, after all, been discovered only two decades before my mother's death. Treatment for diabetes had still been pretty primitive. . .yet there was something peculiar about my mother's end.

It strikes me that Emily might be able to explain this peculiarity. And, even more important, she might be able to tell me what my mother was really like. How pathetic to have to call an absolute stranger to learn about one's own mother. How foolish to have waited so long.

An online phone search quickly locates an Emily Watol in a small town in the Poconos, the only Emily Watol in the country. Thank goodness her married name is not too common.

Invisible hands hold me back—anger at my mother's family, my own dread of being rejected again. I'm totally immobilized for five minutes, and then I force every thought from my mind except Emily's telephone number. Like an automaton, I dial.

Four rings, followed by the cracked tones of an older woman, slightly guarded, startled by the phone's summons.

"Yes?"

I tell her I'm a voice from the past; I used to be Sara Jean Sonkin. What I don't say is that I feel like little Sara Jean, again, praying I won't be shut out, hoping she's got a magic tree with the answers I seek.

She's so slow to respond, I wonder if she's going to hang up, but finally Emily says she's glad I called. I've been on her mind for many years. "I always wondered about you and how you survived that mess." She could be referring to my mother's death from diabetes, my father's suicide, their marital relationship, which was clearly "messy"—all of the above. She sounds so genuinely concerned that I relax and start to imagine what she looks like.

Ages have passed since I last saw Emily, my World War II heroine, yet the image of her pompadour hairdo sticks in my mind. Ridiculous. She must have gone through twenty hairstyles since then, and by now she's surely down to your basic senior citizen trim—no need for high style in the Poconos. But I can't budge her out of the 1940s. She's there along with blackout drills, ration books, 78-rpm records of patriotic fervor—"Let's remember Pearl Harbor, as we go to meet the foe/ let's remember Pearl Harbor, as we did the Alamo."

Songs of the Forties, the first lessons I learned from the radio, run through my head as Emily recounts her story.

After the war, she got a master's degree in chemistry, married ("Well, what do you know, he smiled at me in my dreams last night"), had children ("Mairzy doats and dozy doats and liddle lamzy divey, a kiddley divey too, wouldn't you?") worked for a laboratory, divorced ("I'll walk alone, because to tell you the truth, I'll be lonely"), and finally retired to an old farmhouse with crannies and creaks that suit her ("There's a small hotel, with a wishing well"). Her sister, Anna, seven years older and closer in age to my mother, is a retired professor of history and a widow ("I don't want to walk without you"). She has one son. Emily has two sons. ("Went to the doctor, the doctor said / give those chillums some shortnin' bread.")

The radio switches off, and it's my turn. As I talk about my family, I can hear the wheels turning in Emily's head—*why has Sara Jean called?*

Cancer, that's the ostensible reason. I tell Emily about my gene discovery. "We always wondered why there was so much cancer in the family," she says. Her sister, Anna, had breast cancer seventeen years ago. Her father died young of cancer, and then there was Minnie, my grandmother.

Emily remembers visiting Minnie in a summer bungalow and finding her quite ill. When Emily suggested seeing a doctor, Minnie replied, "I don't want to spoil anyone's vacation." Only later, when Minnie was totally "doped up" and close to death, did Emily learn what the problem was. "In those days, you didn't tell anyone about cancer. It was a deep, dark secret."

I reflect it was a secret Minnie bore for more than a decade, with no support groups, pink ribbon marches, or celebrity speeches. I want to put my arms about Minnie; I want to embrace her entire family.

Minnie was the middle child of Sholem and Sarah, Emily tells me. The youngest was Abe, the father of Anna and Emily. The oldest was Mollie, who had no children.

Mollie, the figure I saw in my dream, was a genuine hysteric, always spinning at dervish speed. At Abe's funeral, Mollie leaped into the open grave and kicked the gravediggers as they tried to lift her out. There was mud on her face and in her mouth and she was still screaming.

It was a traumatic sight for a bereaved little girl like Emily, just eight years old.

I ask myself whether Mollie behaved the same way at my mother's funeral, which I didn't attend. Not being present at either of my parents' funerals made it more difficult for me to accept their deaths. Visiting the cemetery, I couldn't get over the idea that they weren't really there; the neat footstones belonged to other people, imposter bodies, as in the movies, while my parents, inexplicably, were hiding.

That's what I think about now as Emily talks about my mother, her voice, so distant at first, aglow with warmth. "She was a beautiful woman, and bright, too. I hope you look like her."

"I hope so, too," I murmur, but there's not a chance. My mother was blonde and fair; I'm dark, like my father and the other Sonkins. Even as an infant, I looked like a gypsy foundling in my mother's arms.

Gently, I raise the subject of my mother's final illness, reminding Emily that my mother stayed with her before being admitted to the sanitarium where she died. I say I always wondered how my mother could have died of diabetes in a mental facility.

A long pause.

Maybe my question strikes Emily as odd. I can't know that I've struck a nerve.

"Well, she had a couple of bad experiences," Emily responds at last.

That's putting it mildly. A year previously, her husband had killed himself. She was alone in the world, responsible for a bizarre father and an emotionally charged child. But these aren't the "bad experiences" Emily is going to tell me about.

"Your mother was raped by the superintendent of the building in which you were living," she says.

My heart pounds, the bright sunlight fades, yet I keep my voice steady, my fingers clenched around the receiver. ". . . Oh, really."

"Yes. She called to have the kitchen sink fixed, or something like that, and he took advantage of her." All that strikes me at first is Emily's nineteenth-century language, "took advantage of her." I remember the sink and the rust-colored pipe beneath it. And the soap powder we kept nearby. Did he knock over the boxes when he pushed her down?

Emily says that, after she was raped, my mother became depressed and went to stay with her brother, Bernie, and his wife, Theresa, and she also stayed, for a while, with the sisters in Forest Hills.

"She had to get away from her apartment. She was so fragile, anyway, and then to have something like that happen, even for a so-called healthy person it would have been terrible," Emily says.

Emily remembers the exact moment my mother told her about her rape. She was standing on the landing of the staircase at Forest Hills, her shoulders shaking. "Her body had been violated, and she was so vulnerable," Emily remembers sadly. "There was nothing to say."

Nothing to say!—*gevalt!* Run to the rape crisis center (there weren't any), the police (they'd ask for witnesses), the landlord (he'd want witnesses, too). Call *PM*, the left-wing crusading newspaper my mother reads so devotedly. But my mother's run-of-the-mill rape wouldn't qualify as a social crisis, not in 1946, anyway. Then it was just another matter to be kept under wraps, like breast cancer and, like cancer, it ate her away.

Despite my tumultuous thoughts, I keep my voice steady, as if Emily is telling me about a stranger, and in a way, that's so. Yes, it must have been so sad. Oh, I'm so glad she had you to turn to. What a terrible time it must have been.

I murmur on, until we part, after agreeing that I'll visit soon. I have some old photographs of my mother that seem to have been torn from an album. Many include people I don't know. Perhaps Emily can identify them.

My father is not to be seen in any of the pictures. Before he killed himself, he destroyed every scrap of paper pertaining to him. Maybe that's why he's missing from my mother's collection; maybe he was never in it.

After hanging up, I'm numb, unable to move. I cry out for Solomon, and he races into the room, holds me close, and listens to the story. Although he's never said so, I know he doesn't approve of my research, fearing it will only open up old wounds. His job in my life, to smooth and sustain, will grow more difficult.

But even as I snuggle close, my shock is combined with the exhilaration of discovery. I've always been an inveterate researcher, obsessed with a need to know, and now I can see the need relates to the early "mess." I must get closer to that simmering cauldron, even at the risk of falling in.

The next day, while I'm wondering what to do next, the phone rings. It's Emily's older sister, Anna, the retired historian.

Her voice is higher pitched than Emily's, and it has a deliberately cultivated air, like a film star of the 1930s who's been coached in speech.

Anna, too, says that she's always "wondered" about me. "I was so fond of your mother. She was very good to me when we were younger. But after she died, you were kidnapped by the Sonkin family."

Kidnapped? The Sonkins held me close, but I don't think they forbade my mother's relatives to call. After my mother died, there was an additional "mess," a custody battle between her brother, Bernie, and my father's brother, Robert. It ended with the court appointing them joint guardians, but I lived with the Sonkins, and I never saw Bernie, never even got a birthday card. Surely he was entitled to visitation privileges, had he wanted any. Rather than "kidnapped," I felt rescued, abandoned by my mother's relatives.

Anna's spin gives me some pause. Perhaps she'd been shut out, rather than neglectful; perhaps she's merely justifying herself.

Anna is eager to talk about the Podonoff family, particularly her own childhood, which I learn was sad indeed.

Anna's mother, Rachel, was an invalid, suffering from what would be diagnosed today as multiple sclerosis. After Abe's death, Anna and Emily were raised by their maternal grandmother in the Forest Hills house.

Desperately poor (the house was the only asset Abe left), Rachel appealed to the Podonoff relatives repeatedly for money. Mollie advised that she get out of bed and go to work. Minnie helped out when she could. Later, when she was grown, my mother helped, too. I can't imagine that Louis, the miser, sympathized with these efforts, but his women had a wondrous way of slipping money past him—in this case, to the house behind the magic tree.

For Anna, the heroine of the tale is Rachel, brave and beautiful, a victim. I listen politely, but I resent Anna's chatter. I want to hear about my mother, not Rachel.

My mind is racing ahead to how I can get the goods on that superintendent. If there are old records for our apartment building, I'm going to find them, no matter how deeply buried. I don't figure the creature's alive, but I want to connect him to a name; I want to know who would assault a fragile woman, my woman, just because he thought he could get away with it.

At last, Anna gets around to my mother. I say how sorry I was to hear from Emily about the rape.

There's a moment of puzzlement. "Well, that wasn't exactly the story," Anna remarks.

She recalls my mother's stay in Forest Hills. "She was standing on the landing when she turned to tell me something. She said she'd been seeing a psychiatrist and somehow ended up in his bed. She was lonely and vulnerable after your father died, and he took advantage of her." The same setting and the same words Emily used to describe the rapist.

But Anna is certain of her version. "I remember because it was so shocking, given the morality of the time. Your mother must have seen the expression on my face—she looked away." Anna never forgot the way my mother closed the conversation. "She murmured, '*You* didn't think I was like that, did you?'"

Anna's carefully modulated voice is rising now. "She feared I might think less of her. But I never blamed her. I blamed the man."

"The man" was an eminent psychiatrist, the head of a professional organization, beyond reproach. In those days, women didn't accuse important doctors of sexual abuse any more than they talked about breast cancer or being raped.

Many years later, at the college where Anna taught, a professor was taking sexual advantage of his students. Anna led a faculty battle to discipline the man. "I had to do it. I remembered your mother," she says.

Anna tells me how my mother wound up staying in Forest Hills. She had been with Bernie and Theresa, but apparently Bernie called and said he needed a vacation. "Can you and Emily take Clara for a while?"

"Your mother couldn't be left alone, so of course we said yes, but I could never figure out why he had to go away just then," says Anna nervously.

I can hear she's still annoyed with Bernie after all these years. But why? Surely he'd been entitled to a break. And when he got back, he'd had to admit my mother to West Hill Sanitarium because her diabetes went out of control. Or had he? Perhaps the sisters had made the arrangements and resented doing what they thought was Bernie's job.

There's some evidence for this in what Anna tells me next.

The day my mother died, Grandpa Louis appeared in Forest Hills, blue eyes flashing. He'd traveled from the Bronx, paying two full fares, subway and bus, normally unthinkable.

Tapping Anna's shoulder, he'd shouted, "What did you do to my Clara? She was fine when she came here."

Louis went on castigating Anna; then he did something else. He offered to sell her my mother's fur coats. "Imagine, she was scarcely dead, and he was selling her coats." Anna turned him down, but Louis probably managed to sell the coats elsewhere, she says. That's how focused he was on money.

Memories of Louis upset Anna. Gently, I steer the conversation back to the present, her retirement, her son and granddaughter, and then, a final promise to keep in touch.

But hours after hanging up the phone, Louis's accusatory words to Anna haunt me. "What did you do to my Clara?" Was he simply wild with grief, or had something actually been 'done' to my mother?

A few days later, Aunt Sylvia, who knows I've been searching for my mother's cousins, asks if I've found

Anna and Emily. I fill her in, but I don't say what they told me about my mother. I do reveal that I'm planning to visit Emily in the Poconos.

Sylvia looks upset. She regards Emily as an outsider.

"Can't you just *write* to Emily?" Sylvia asks.

I shake my head, but Sylvia doesn't notice my refusal; she's remembering something. "When your mother was staying with them, we talked on the phone a few times, and she told me they took her to a doctor," Sylvia murmurs.

Probably for therapy, I reply, since she was depressed.

"No, another kind of a doctor, a gynecologist, I think. She had some kind of vaginal infection."

I can't believe what Sylvia is saying. I leap to a conclusion. My mother had the kind of infection that takes nine months to clear up. She became pregnant by either the superintendent or the psychiatrist, and Anna and Emily tried to help. They helped because Bernie ducked out ("I don't know why he had to go away just then"), because my mother used to slip money to their invalid mother, because they loved her.

As a child, I was possessed by the desire to have a sibling. I never thought about the down side, the sibling rivalry side.

A good friend had a sadistic teenage sister who beat her when their parents weren't home. Once, when I was visiting, the sister pushed my friend down on the sofa and started to smother her, until I started screaming real loud; but *my* sibling wouldn't do something like that. A sister would be like Josephine March in *Little Women*, a brother like Laurie, the Marches' adorable neighbor. My sibling would be younger than I was, of course, but somehow, older, too—nurturing, while needing my care.

I pestered my mother to have a baby. She said that, to deliver me, she'd had to have an operation called a Cesarean, because of her diabetes. It was only safe to have a Cesarean once. It sounded ominous, and I got the picture. Diabetes and having babies didn't mix. I was going to remain a loner.

Still, I longed for her to get pregnant, to see her belly turn into a solid balloon like so many of the neighbor ladies', bizarre, yet wonderful.

How ironic that the superintendent or the doctor might have provided the sibling I wanted. Perhaps a tiny life was pulsating when my mother paused on the landing and asked Anna, "You didn't think I was like that, did you?"

But why did Anna and Emily hear two different things on the landing? They're advanced in years, perhaps confused, though both sound sharp as tacks.

I consider the possibilities:

Emily feared I'd think ill of my mother if I knew she had an affair, so she invented the rape.

Anna feared I'd be shocked by the violence of rape, so she invented the affair.

My mother, a former mental patient, made up both stories.

I can tell that Solomon leans toward the latter theory, because these stories are too weird for words. But my mother as fantasist defies everything I remember about her. Rather than making up stories, she leaned heavily toward rationalism. When I begged for a sibling, she gave me the medical facts. When I asked about death, she said there was no after-life. When I wanted to believe in Santa Claus, she told me he didn't exist. "He's just a spirit that people make up to encourage kindness," she said. "Stories like that are nice, but they're not true."

Making up rapists had to be worse than making up Santa Claus.

And then there was Sylvia's memory of an infection and Louis's accusation—*What did you do to my Clara?*

I think back to my conversation with Emily. There was no reason for her to tell me anything about my mother's death. She could have said, "I don't know what happened." Instead, she told me a story that had been weighing on her mind for decades, even as she "wondered" what became of me.

It was as if the sisters had been waiting for me to call, waiting to have a burden lifted.

I remember Emily's words: "Well, she had a few bad experiences."

A few would allow for both the superintendent and the psychiatrist.

The super raped her, making her more vulnerable to the psychiatrist. The psychiatrist seduced her, making her more vulnerable to the superintendent.

And both of these experiences make my mother's departure wearing that mouton coat more explicable to me. I always thought she disappeared of her own free will; she didn't love me enough to stay. Depression wasn't enough of an explanation for her go away permanently. Most likely, my being unlovable was the problem.

But suddenly I see my mother as an abused woman, a woman too fragile to stand up to the blows life had thrown at her. She didn't leave me; abuse pried her away, drove her into the ground.

My mother lacked a champion, but now I'm in a position to correct that situation. By defending her, I can bring her closer, show her that she didn't have to die on me. I can justify my very existence.

Her abusers are back there in 1946, perfectly safe in an era that would have judged my mother, not them. She bore the shame ("You didn't know I was like that, did you?"), while they continued to go about their business.

But I'm not going to let them get away it. Writing is

a time machine; bang on the keyboard long enough, and you catch up with the past. Bang on the keyboard long enough, and you get your revenge.

I'm going to get my hands on these two guys, rake them over the coals, just the way Anna did with the lascivious professor. I'm going to dig up them up and haul their ghost asses into court. Just watch me.

3
The Year 1946

I CALL UPON THE DEAD to give evidence. I saw this happen in *The Dybbuk*, a classic Yiddish play about spirit possession. In the play, a rabbi summons a witness from the next world to a rabbinical court.

It isn't easy. A messenger has to be sent to the cemetery to command the dead man's presence. The rabbi must draw a circle on the floor to contain the spirit witness, and then put up a sheet to separate the living from the dead.

I have neither the moral power of the rabbi nor his kabbalistic skills, but I do have a sheet and a dank basement where apparitions are likely.

The sheet is worn, a fitted twin that's seen too many nights in the guest room, but it can separate two worlds as well as any other. I hang it on an old clothesline, and

I bang on the cement floor with a vacuum cleaner hose:

> *You, superintendent of 1520 Sheridan Avenue, Bronx, in the year 1946, come at once. Something needs to be fixed.*
>
> *You, eminent psychiatrist, probably of Park Avenue in the year 1946, come at once. Someone needs to be fixed.*

Is it my imagination, or does the sheet shudder slightly? It's suddenly aglow, luminescent, even though the color was washed out years ago.

Through the light, I seem to see a man's broad shoulders, and I conjure up the rest—blonde-gray hair, protruding teeth, a ready smile. Conjuring, or did I know this man as a child? I would have passed him as I raced down the steps armed with jacks, a Spaldine ball, or a jump rope. I would have seen him carrying paint cans, a tool box, or a mop.

In Bronx buildings, supers were always going somewhere. Not enough heat? Dumbwaiter broken? Call the super. Sometimes you might have to "make nice," slip him some money, so that he came to your apartment first, ahead of those other tenants, whose demands were less vital.

"She didn't call much," a voice says suddenly. "She could fix a lot of things herself." That day, though, there was a problem with the kitchen sink, or maybe it was the stove or the radiator, so I came right away, he says.

Well, mister, it doesn't matter what needed fixing; you did the job, and then you raped her. She probably enticed you by saying something nice like "thank you," and then there was no way of stopping you. You were pushing her down, pulling off her slacks, pulling up her skirt, tearing off her underpants. You shoved your penis into her vagina and thrust back and forth, a grunting, thirsting animal. "Don't say anything," you whispered. She could feel the weight of your body, a meteorite inexplicably fallen from the sky. You kept going while she struggled to understand how it had happened.

You hurt her—bruises on her neck and shoulders from the kitchen floor. As for her mind, you pulverized it, pushing her into a permanent black hole. Did her vulnerability tempt you, a woman alone, a woman whose wacko husband had committed suicide? Maybe she's a wacko, too. Let's find out.

"She offered me a cup of coffee," he says. "That means she wanted it bad. No one in that building ever gave me anything for nothing."

So it's the *Lady Chatterley's Lover* defense—lascivious lady of the manor, downtrodden muscular servant. Poor me, they only love me for my prick.

I'm not buying, because I've read about the year 1946 and I know that supers were doing pretty well. That year,

Local 21, Apartment House Superintendents Union, American Federation of Labor, won a great contract—a $10 increase, bringing wages to $46 a week, better than schoolteachers', who, after all, were only women. Still, my mother undoubtedly applauded the contract, as she did all gains for working people, and then this super walked into her apartment, raped her, and offers excuses. Well, fuck him, and, while you're at it, fuck the whole year 1946.

In that first post-war year, the world was supposed to be headed for peace. We sang about it in school: "The hope of humanity singing /A hymn to a new world in birth."

But the "new world" never managed to get born, even with the United Nations as midwife. National groups continued to pursue their bad old ways and bad old attitudes continued to exist about most things, including women.

In 1946, cultures far and wide stigmatized rape victims. In Bengal, India, the scene of Hindu-Moslem warfare, the rape figures were too high to calculate. Mohandas K.Gandhi, human rights advocate, exhorted Hindu women to commit suicide rather than submit to dishonor. He even told them how to do it: Hold your breath until you suffocate. Later, learning this was medically impossible, he suggested taking poison instead.

Pretty tough to swallow poison when your enemies are sweeping into your village, when they have you by the throat. But Gandhi wasn't interested in mechanics, just in making sure women knew the shame was theirs.

In New York City, in 1946, rape, while troubling, was not a crime that carried a heavy penalty. The case of Jack Colletti and Phil Fusco, two Lower East Side "thugs," was unusual. They got five-to-ten-year sentences for the attempted rape of a WAC in a tenement hallway. The judge said his severity was prompted by the fact that the victim was wearing the uniform of the United States Army.

Almost all of the rapists described in *New York Times* stories were "thugs," "hoodlums" or "Negroes." Without a witness, no woman would report a respectable man, a man without a criminal record, a white man. Her credibility would be zero. The mores of the time gave the superintendent *carte blanche* to "take advantage" of my mother.

Even so, he deserves a special place in Hell. He encountered a woman in mourning, struggling to put her life back together, and he ripped her apart. Down he goes, deep into Dante territory, this regular guy with his nifty union contract and his unbridled lust.

The super's pretty easy to deal with, a creep after all. But the other "criminal," my mother's seducer, he's so smooth. Right now he's standing behind my judgment sheet, smoking a pipe, looking through his progress notes, smoothing down the lapels of his tweed jacket. The big-wheel psychiatrist.

I can hear his breathing and an occasional cough; maybe he's reaching for a tissue from the box he keeps for pitiful patients.

Finally, he speaks. He's booked weeks ahead, he says, the laws of heaven and earth can't change that—and I haven't got an appointment. More important, he can't talk with me, ever, because the doctor-patient relationship is confidential. He's sure I understand.

I can't help smiling. His type of relationship was very confidential, perhaps for many years. "She wound up in his bed," Anna said, implying more than occasional *shtupping* on the therapeutic couch.

I try to imagine the man who would mess with a patient's mind this way.

If he was a psychoanalyst, he was probably European-born, like most New York analysts at the time. Perhaps he was trained by Sigmund Freud himself or by one of his adherents, Otto Rank, Karl Abraham, Sandor Ferenzci, or Hanns Sachs.

It's easy to guess that he was brilliant, insightful, dominating—words that describe a number of Freud's followers. In 1946, these men were gods, a status they accepted as appropriate, giant egos matched to giant brains. It would have been inconceivable for a patient to accuse such a doctor of sexual exploitation. Who would have believed her? As with rape, she was left to internalize the guilt.

It wasn't until the 1980s, when my mother was long dead, that women began to bring charges. In one famous case, Barbara Noel, a singer, sued Dr. Jules H. Masserman, chairman of the psychiatry department at Northwestern Medical School. Masserman was highly revered by the profession, and he continued to receive honors, even as Noel and other victims charged that he gave them the drug Amytal in therapy and then raped them as they slept. It took years, and the settlement of several civil suits, before the American Psychiatric Association suspended Masserman and he resigned his license.

Even today, it's difficult for the psychiatric profession to police itself. In 1946, the profession didn't have to bother. How easy it must have been for the doctor to weave his spell.

My mother is a woman alone. Years ago, she broke free of the Jewish religion, and in its stead, installed the new god—psychiatry. She worships the doctor's ability to provide answers, like Jehovah on high. She trusts him absolutely.

I imagine that, in their sessions, she reveals anger toward her dead husband, murderous wishes toward her miserly father, frustration in dealing with her child, lingering sorrow over her mother's death. He nods, writes it down, reeks with empathy.

He says she needs to raise her self-esteem. He hands her a tissue and smiles in a fatherly fashion, or what she takes to be a fatherly fashion, since her own father rarely smiles.

It seems to me that, one day, my mother tells the doctor about a dream, her mother, Minnie, getting on a train. The train vanishes into the distance, becoming smaller and smaller, as my mother's calls for Minnie go unanswered. My mother wakes up sobbing, unable to bear this message of final separation.

In the office, she weeps anew—agitated, gets up from the couch, and walks around. Despite her light clothing, cotton dress, and sandals, she's feverish, as if inviting the cool touch of his hand and then—the floor, the couch, the desk—where it happens doesn't matter. The barrier breaks at incredible speed, light years of neediness.

Let's give him a break. Let's say he has genuine feelings for her. Or maybe he's just a bottom-line narcissist, consumed by his own ego.

One way or the other, she's his.

At first, my mother feels flattered, validated. But she's confused, too. He assures her the affair is beautiful, even therapeutic. Doesn't she believe she deserves a love like his? She shouldn't think so little of herself. They'll have to discuss her feelings of unworthiness in therapy.

It goes on—needing, doubting, needing again.

I imagine that one month she misses a menstrual period, and the next month, again. She tells herself it's early menopause, common in diabetics, but she knows the truth.

Dread turns her into an automaton, writing lesson plans without thinking, dressing without noticing what she puts on. She can't remember the conversations she has with her child or her father.

At night, when her mind clears a little, she thinks back to her first pregnancy, the one she had been warned against.

"It's way too dangerous for a diabetic," Anna told me her doctor had argued when she told him she wanted to get pregnant. He hammered out the facts—forty-five percent of the babies of diabetic women are stillborn, maternal deaths common.

She refused to listen. Motherhood would bolster her marriage, comfort her ailing mother, validate her life. My father was frightened, but he agreed because she was so obsessed, and for nine months, he scarcely took a breath. After delivery, she experienced convulsions, his worst fears realized. But she recovered, emerging triumphant from the lion's den, her cub in tow.

This new pregnancy is something different, a badge of shame. Have the child, and the whole world will know she's "like that." She'll lose her job, her status, maybe even her little girl. She needs to find a solution.

The year 1946 was a rotten time to be raped or seduced by your doctor, but it was an even worse time to be seeking an abortion.

Until then, abortion, though illegal in most states, had been pretty much condoned. Doctors who didn't perform abortions discreetly referred patients to others who did. But in the middle of the 1940s, widespread crackdowns on "abortion mills" began. Every doctor who made a referral risked prosecution for being a "steerer." Every woman who turned to a "mill" risked falling into the hands of the police.

There were plenty of mills around. Not too far from our Bronx apartment, a Dr. Brandenberg and his partners, Mr. and Mrs. Strauss, ran an operation worth $500,000 a year, according to the *New York Times*.

In 1946, even as my mother might have made an appointment with Brandenberg or someone like him, the district attorney's office was on the prowl. Female police officers, posing as women "in trouble," infiltrated the Strauss mill. They found out the names of the "steerers"; they learned when abortions were likely to be performed.

It took the assistant district attorney a year to gather all the evidence. Then, one morning, he personally burst through the Strauss doors, followed by a pack of police and reporters. The raiders found five cowering women, three "already treated" and two "waiting their turn."

Imagine, you've just come off the abortionist's table, weak and bleeding, you didn't get too much anesthetic, maybe none at all, your emotions in turmoil, when suddenly a door slams, and you're confronted by a district attorney, a young man on the way up at your expense. Or maybe you're "waiting your turn," too frightened to even imagine what's coming next, when suddenly. . . .

If you were "already treated," you were taken to Lincoln Hospital. If you were "waiting your turn," you were taken to the Bronx Park Precinct. In either place, you undoubtedly got badgered, because that was the practice, to stick it to the woman: "Who steered you to the doctor?"

"What's the name of the guy who got you pregnant?"

"Does your mother know about this?"

Later on, you might be asked to name the abortionist in court. Your name, of course, would be printed in the newspapers.

Worse than disgrace, abortion could result in death, because treating complications had become risky for physicians. Earlier, it was common to admit the woman to the hospital with a diagnosis of miscarriage or some other condition. Traditionally, New York City hospitals accepted these fictions, even though they were legally required to report suspected criminal practice. But in the mid-1940s, as part of the abortion crackdown, law enforcement agencies began to scrutinize hospital records. Hospitals could no longer easily provide cover.

If something went wrong, it could be good-bye for both the woman and her doctor, no matter how well connected.

In October 1947, a young woman anonymously visited the office of Paul Singer, a fashionable Park Avenue gynecologist, and begged him for "help."

It's difficult to believe that Singer needed this kind of business. Most likely he felt genuinely sorry for the twenty-two-year-old. He asked a colleague, Oswald Glasberg, an East Side plastic surgeon, to aid him in performing an abortion.

A few days later, the young woman returned to Singer's office, suffering from complications. A less responsible abortionist might simply have turned her away. Abortionists who were not medical doctors had little choice but to do this. Singer admitted his patient to Park East Hospital, where he was ultimately unsuccessful at covering up the real reasons for her condition.

Despite Singer's efforts, the young woman died a

week later. By then he'd learned that she was Jane Ward, heiress to the Ward baking empire. The Ward name made the case front-page news. After three high-profile trials for manslaughter, Singer went to prison and Glasberg committed suicide. Glasberg's wife said she was glad he didn't have to suffer anymore. Women who died from abortion complications, agonizing peritonitis, must have been glad to die, too.

Every woman "in trouble" knew that she could wind up like Jane Ward, whether she visited a Bronx abortion mill or a Park Avenue doctor. Every doctor knew that he could wind up like Singer, Brandenberg, and the others.

I can't be certain my mother had an abortion in 1946. My only evidence is a cousin's memory of an affair and an aunt's memory of a vaginal infection. Also, the fact that my mother died at West Hill, a sanitarium ill-equipped to treat a patient for diabetic complications. My mother's admission to West Hill makes the most sense if diabetes was the cover story for abortion complications. West Hill would have been less likely than a medical hospital to attract the attention of the law.

I go to the library of the New York Medical Society and examine a medical directory from the 1940s. In the brief listing for West Hill, I read that all the doctors were psychiatrists, with the exception of a cardiologist, undoubtedly on staff to monitor electric shock treatment.

The cardiologist is the man who signed my mother's death certificate, stating he had treated her for diabetic complications.

My mother might have had a prior relationship with West Hill. It could have been the place where she was treated for "sadness" years earlier—Aunt Sylvia remembered the name of that institution had a "West" in it. If so, West Hill might have been inclined to do an ex-patient a favor.

Or maybe it was just treating the ex-patient for the same old problem, depression. But then, why describe diabetic complications as the admitting problem? Why have a cardiologist say he'd been treating my mother for diabetes for the entire five days she was there?

Affair, infection, out-of-the-limelight sanitarium, they all seem to go together.

They fit with 1946, the dreadful year that took my mother from me, the year when so many things had to be hidden—cancer, rape, seduction, abortion, truth of every kind—truth so deeply concealed I can only depend on gut instinct to sort it out.

My instinct sees my mother as a victim, a widow at thirty-nine, dead at forty. Something, someone, has to be responsible; otherwise I wouldn't have been hurt so much. For the moment, I choose the superintendent, the psychiatrist, and what they "did" to her. I choose abortion, though well aware I may be making it up.

Only this time, she won't have to go through the procedure alone. I'll be the comforter she lacked in 1946, the sage who understands the hypocrisy of the era, the daughter-mother who loves her.

That's why I see myself sitting in a doctor's office, waiting for her to be "already treated," biting my nails, feeling illicit, as the times require me to feel.

It's late afternoon, and there's not another soul in the place, except for the police officers I imagine hovering at the door. If they break in, I'm prepared to kick, bite, and scream, just like little Sara Jean working over the family doctor. If I make enough trouble, they'll take me to the station house instead of her.

Yes, you bastards, I'm her "steerer." I'm trying to steer her to safety, peace, whatever it takes to get over what's troubling her, whatever it takes to keep her with me. Why aren't you out looking for rapists instead of harassing frightened women?

The police never show. It's too hot. In the subway, riders swelter in overcrowded cars. In the parks, bench sitters fan themselves with folded newspapers.

In the treatment room, as hot as every other place, the doctor completes the procedure. Into the waste pail goes the sibling I always wanted, a tiny mass of tissue, an intermingling of the mother's genes and whose—the brilliant analyst, the lascivious superintendent? Clean-up of patient and garbage is accomplished in no time. The doctor has to work fast.

"You can come in now," he says.

My mother is seated on the examining table, shivering despite the heat. I wrap a clean sheet around her shoulders. Then I look away because I don't want her to see that I am crying.

No chance of that; she's still pretty groggy from the anesthetic.

The doctor hands me a prescription and says she must remember to take the sulfa pills at the stated intervals. He's sorry he doesn't have antibiotics, but they're not widely available yet. Until they are, abortion will remain unsafe, so my mother has to be careful. She should wear sanitary napkins until the bleeding stops and not move around too much. Plenty of rest is advisable.

If she develops a fever or severe nausea, I should call him immediately. I ask what he'd do then, but he refuses to say. I know he would send my mother to a hospital on some pretext or other, washing his hands of the business as quickly as possible.

He's eager for us to leave, but I insist that my mother lie down for a while in the waiting room. He hovers about, and I can only hope he's done a good job. I pray he's not jinxed like Singer, Glasberg, and Brandenberg.

When my mother feels better, I guide her through the lobby and into the street. A cab arrives, unbidden, a gigantic 1946 Checker, headlights flashing. There's plenty of room—that was the name of the game with Checkers—but I can't settle in. No matter where I sit, the hot leather burns, forcing me back to the sidewalk, a stranger once more. All I can do is make sure my mother is comfortable. I shove the prescription into her pocket, kiss her ashen face, and give the scowling driver two addresses, those of Bernie and Theresa, and of Anna and Emily.

I don't know where he takes her, but within the next few weeks, the dreaded complication occurs. My mother develops a severe infection—"what did you do to Clara?"—and one of the relatives has her admitted to West Hill Sanitarium in Riverdale.

As for the rapist and the seducer, they get off Scott-free; of course they do; this is 1946.

Did he visit her at West Hill, the guilty party, express his sorrow, regret, penitence? Did he ask about her little girl and how she would cope?

I want to make him do those things, clobber him with the scales of justice. And then I remember the other-worldly court I've erected, using a sheet as battered and bruised as my mother.

I stare at the sheet and hear a strained cough, the psychiatrist waiting for my attention. Undoubtedly, my meandering bores him. He hears so many sad stories. I'm causing him to miss billable hours, if it's possible to send bills from hell.

"You're upset," he says, in the smooth tone that won her trust. "Too bad your anger is misplaced."

I want to rip down the sheet and punch him out, but I don't say a word.

He goes on. "Surely you've heard of *projection*. You're transferring your anger at someone else to me. After all, I'm not the one who should have been protecting her. There's a man missing. He's the guilty party, if you had the guts to admit it. You can't know the truth about her until you've dealt with *him*."

Damn it—the doctor's got a point.

I rip down the sheet and stare into the dark basement, searching for the missing man, as I have for so many years. No need to command his presence; he's always hovering near—my father, my poor father—perpetually guilty, but never imagining the crime I'm laying on him now.

I summon my memories, bang on the floor with the vacuum cleaner hose. I hear shuffling, someone drawing near, tentative, maybe wearing bedroom slippers to soften his presence, the way he did with his existence. Barely there to the world, except for me, to whom he was everything. I hold my breath, and I can almost see him. Here he comes, my dear one, on trial for the life he never had.

4

My Father At The Bar

MY FATHER WAS THE great love of my life, my little life. I thought the sun rose and set on him, but I didn't expect the sun to set so soon. He threw himself downward into the earth like an Aztec god defying gravity. But I didn't see it that way. I thought the earth simply gobbled him up, the pure of heart, into its sinister core. That how it had to have happened, because he was so reliable, I set my clock by him; I set my heart by him.

My earliest memory is that the world *is* him; he's all around, making me safe, sharing himself. We're bound tied together like Siamese twins, on our own planet, because my mother is often away, or often they're not together—I don't know how it happens, but it's two for the road. We're walking in the park while he sings his favorite song, "April Showers"; we're on a trolley car, going to visit his parents, and he explains how men from far away in Italy laid the tracks many decades ago. We're on the beach at Far Rockaway, where Grandpa Louis rented a summer bungalow. My father comes on weekends, like other Jewish husbands whose toil guards their families from monstrous heat and polio epidemics. I watch my father walking down the iron steps of the elevated train station, seersucker jacket folded neatly over his arm, a bag of promised beach toys in his hand for me. He's always buying me things; whatever I ask for, whatever I dream of, he gets it. Industry is in war production; there aren't many toys being made, and that's fortunate, or he'd be broke. He's a walking candy store.

On Rockaway Beach, it's better than a candy store, the air so delicious you could eat it—the crusty smells of sun-drenched boardwalk and dancing ocean spray, the never-ending light, the magic sand that enables you to build marvels, castles where princesses languish, bridges that span the sky, ships that sail past tomorrow. When you're done building, you dig a big hole, lie down, cover yourself with sand, and gaze into the endless sky. The deeper the hole, the damper the sand, the more you sneeze, and you giggle, too, because you know that soon he'll find you, dig you out, and give you a hug. And then, the two of you head for the water's edge. You watch the waves rolling in, rumbling like volcanoes, and he picks you up and holds you safely above him with one hand as he dives through a wave. On the shore, other little kids scream and run away as the water licks their heels, but you laugh and beg him to go out further, because everything is so dark blue, so inviting, and you know there isn't any wave big enough to conquer him. He's a fine swimmer, and you vow to be a fine swimmer, too, because nothing is as glorious as being in the water with him.

But the glory ended early, and there was a reason for that. My sweet father was too good for this world, because he wanted nothing for himself, thought little of himself, and those are the signs of a really fine person, according to his family, the Sonkins. To this day, at the Passover *seder*, when we read the allegory of the Four Sons—one wise and good, one wicked, one simple, and one unable to ask questions—Aunt Sylvia remarks, "Your father was the good son."

He left this world because no psychiatrist could help him live in it; he killed himself to protect his family from the awful things he invented that he had done. And it's ironic, because he was really the best, the brightest, of his three bright siblings, and no one knew it except for his family and a few colleagues at work. His lifelong desire to efface himself, which culminated in suicide, was the crowning achievement of his virtue—and I was his offspring.

Away from the ocean, I was a timorous child, but in the months before my father's death, I became a terrified child, hiding my fear with my friends, but a basket case at night. I would wake in the dark, my body covered with perspiration, my mind screaming with fear. In the closet there was a horrible monster, not the comic book kind that frightens you, but a satanic force, a whirlwind—more powerful than those fighter squadrons that flashed across the sky at the end of war movies. The monster could blow away those squadrons; he could tear the world apart.

When that hit me, how everything could disappear, I'd yell for my father at the top of my lungs. Only he could subdue the monster, the way he did with those waves at Rockaway Beach. After a few weeks of these night terrors, my mother didn't want my father to respond anymore. It wasn't good to get into such a pattern, she argued; the childcare experts said you had to set limits. She'd call my father back, but he stayed in my room, curled up at the foot of the bed, telling me stories until I fell back to sleep.

These stories were the only thing that calmed me down. My father was a history buff. He told me about the French and Indian War and how clever George Washington was to take a clue from the Indians and fight guerilla style—hit and run—rather than face to face on the battlefield with a superior foe. The English generals looked down their fancy noses at Washington's methods, but later they realized he had won the war for them. I had the feeling my father had been there, that's how involved he was in Washington's maneuvers.

Sometimes my father soothed me by suggesting that I picture myself floating on a cloud. This helped him fall asleep, he said, better than counting sheep. If images didn't work, he'd read to me, even though it was late at night. At eight, I was a voracious reader, with a collection of Nancy Drew mysteries and Bobbsey Twin books, but my father's favorite was *Alice in Wonderland.* His copy was a worn volume with a blue cover. The top corner of each page looked nibbled at, since he had a habit, a compulsion really, of tearing off snippets while reading.

I barely understood the world of Wonderland, except that it was upside down, just like my own life. I thought it would be great to meet up with a white rabbit, have loony adventures, and use all the funny-sounding words, but what I really loved with the sound of those words on my father's tongue, soothing me better than a cloud, until I fell asleep.

Early one morning, a short time after an Alice session, I was awakened by my mother's voice, filled with urgency. "My husband has jumped off the roof," she said. I realized that she was on the telephone, talking to the police.

After that, I heard the front door slam, and I pictured

her racing down the stairs to where his crushed body lay. When you jumped off the roof, you were dead, messy dead; you couldn't move, just the way I couldn't move right then. I was paralyzed; the monster had done its work.

Grandpa Louis came into my room, which faced the courtyard, and headed for the window. His white, veined hand was ready to open the Venetian blinds when I screamed for him to stop. I didn't want to see anything outside. My voice sounded funny, upside down, like Alice's voice. To avoid throwing up, I grabbed a Nancy Drew mystery and buried my nose in it. I read the same paragraph over and over.

Suddenly, there was a policeman in the room. In school, we sang a song about how a "kind" policeman could help if you got lost. I was certainly lost. "Are you all right?" he asked, kindly enough. I thought, *I'll be all right when my father gets here,* and then I realized he'd never be able to make things all right again. I'd have to go on without him, accepting no substitutes. Something kept rising in my throat, and I swallowed hard to keep it down. I made a mask of my face. "I'm fine," I told the policeman.

I can't remember who came and went and what happened next. Before my father's funeral, my mother stood in front of her clothes closet, picking out something to wear, tears streaming down her cheeks. She murmured my father's name, "Oh, Daniel." My heart echoed the word: *Daniel, Daniel, Daniel.*

Later, after my mother's death when I went to live with my father's parents, I shared a bedroom with my Grandma Kate. At night, I'd sometimes hear her crying in her sleep, "Daniel." In school, when we sang "Danny Boy" in music appreciation, I thought it was about him, and I'd cry inside, because I never cried out loud—"Daniel."

My Grandma Kate and her siblings all named their first sons Daniel, after their father, who had died at a young age, shortly before Kate set off for America. There was Henya's Daniel, David's Daniel, Ida's Daniel, Sophie's Daniel, and Kate's, Daniel—*my* Daniel. They looked alike, these D-boys—slim frames, dark complexions, deep mysterious eyes gazing out on a world of expectation, the expectations set by Henya, David, Ida, Sophie, Kate, and millions of other immigrants for their children. They should have been named Jacob because they were to climb ladders, the first generation of Jews to benefit from America's opportunity. But that meant measuring up—at school, professions, and marriage. Eyes were always watching, comparing, and particularly Kate's eyes. Within that tight-knit, loving, extended family, there was also fierce competition.

Daniel and his brother, Robert, were bright little sons, always skipping grades, tripping along a golden path. Robert graduated from high school at fourteen, City College, at eighteen. But Kate wasn't satisfied with her children's accomplishments; there was always something missing. Her expectations were enormous, her disappointments a continual sigh, and my father resonated, tuned in like a pitchfork.

My father's childhood comes down to me from Aunt Sylvia, who was eight years his junior. She recalls that he was studious, an avid reader, a pretty good athlete, funny in a quiet way, and not too social. His best friends, maybe his only friends, were cousins within the family. I imagine that he was too tense to be comfortable with outsiders. Even as a child, he must have been focused inward, worrying about meeting expectations, super-anxious. My father undoubtedly suffered from obsessive-compulsive disorder, with its rituals—the only one I know is the page tearing—and the need to have everything "just so," along with a heightened sense of doubt, responsibility, and guilt. His greatest fear was doing something terribly wrong and, in high school, that's what happened.

In his senior year, my father failed a trigonometry course. The failure decimated him so completely that he fled high school, took a civil service exam, and got a job in the post office. With his obsessive concentration, he became an expert at handling dead letters, sorting out where they really belonged. For this, he achieved some degree of recognition, particularly from me.

As a child, I was proud to have a father who worked for the post office because the kind postman, like the kind policeman, figured prominently in my first-grade reader. I didn't realize that, in taking a post office job, my father had settled, walked away from his superior intelligence, hid in a place where he felt safe.

I was in high school when Aunt Sylvia told me why my father left school, and it made perfect sense. I, too, felt humiliated if I got a poor grade, as if I had let my family down. I had never failed a course, but I knew that would be the end of the world. In our family, every action one took was terribly important, with grave consequences, and the worst possible thing was to fail or make a mistake. There was no such thing as "letting go," "moving on," or any other phrase that meant forgetting. We were stuck, revisiting anything that had gone wrong, piling on the reasons for self-blame.

When I grew older and saw that overcoming failure was important, I asked Sylvia why my father hadn't repeated the trigonometry course as often as was necessary to pass. She looked at me in amazement. Apparently, I had misunderstood. He hadn't been perfect; there was no going on after that. It would have been too humiliating to show up in class again, after one had done the terrible thing of failing. And the neighbors would know, and worst of all, the cousins, those other Daniels. Better to slink off quietly, squeezing one's self-esteem into a ball and tossing it away.

I've come to realize that there must have been other reasons, besides the trigonometry failure, for my father's leaving high school. Perhaps school made him too anxious, despite his generally high performance. Perhaps he behaved oddly in some manner I can't imagine. He was a troubled adolescent in search of acceptance. *Voilá* U.S. Post Office. But even as the job met his needs, he looked down on himself for being "just a postal worker." A few years later, the Great Depression struck, and the status of postal worker got upgraded. As the Depression deepened, just having a job made a young man desirable, and a safe government job was at the top of the list.

My father was then in his middle twenties and good looking, judging by old photographs. Apparently, he liked women but didn't date too much. He went to parties with his best friend, a first cousin, and my father spoke so softly, his witty remarks couldn't be heard above the din. The cousin would repeat them for the company. "Did you hear what Daniel just said?" My father smiled quietly, hovering in the background. For him to be present in life, he needed an agent.

He might have needed agents to get married.

Here is what I think could have happened: Philip and Kate began to worry about Daniel's lack of social assertion. The other Daniels may have already been married, so there was no time to waste, marriage being a commandment within the Jewish culture. They saw their Daniel as simply shy, not emotionally troubled, stuck with the most abysmally low self-image of the century. He just needed a push. They looked around within the network they knew best—the family.

Kate's sister, Sophie, was married to Louis' brother, Cassel, so the Sonkins knew the Paleys. The families saw each other occasionally, and sometimes Philip and Louis met at meetings of the Minsker Independent Benevolent Association. Louis had a daughter, Clara, a school teacher; Philip had a son, Daniel, a postal worker. A fine match—it was a *mitzvah*, a good deed, to bring them together.

Great news—they seemed to be attracted to one another. My father's gentle, undemanding demeanor provided a pleasant counterpoint to Louis's relentless egotism. My mother's vivacity and army of friends made Daniel feel alive. With her, his social life would be assured; she'd be a full-time agent.

Philip and Kate were relieved. They didn't know that

Louis and Minnie were relieved, also. They had a reason for wanting to see Clara married, and to a young man who didn't know her too well.

The wedding took place in June 1931. A notice appeared in the next bulletin of the Minsker Independent Benevolent Association, bursting with excitement and undoubtedly place by Philip himself: *To our Brother Philip Sonkin, whose tireless devotion to the M.I.B.A. is priceless, we extend our heartiest congratulations on the marriage of his son, Daniel, to Clara, the daughter of our Bro. Louis Paley. We wish the newlyweds the best of luck, and hope Daniel will emulate his father in the M.I.B.A.* Philip's "hope" was in the nature of a command. Minsker membership was falling off; the immigrants' children, more secure in America, had less need of a buffer organization. But Daniel would heed the injunction to join. He was the "good son," intent on fulfilling the expectations of others.

Best of luck, said Philip's message, but luck had already run out. On a honeymoon cruise to Nova Scotia, my mother fell ill. Seated on a deck chair, her head would slump forward, and she'd almost black out. Or they'd be having dinner, and she'd become woozy, her conversation unintelligible. My father was terrified. My mother had sometimes suffered similar "spells" when they were dating, driving in her brother Bernie's car, for example, but they lifted quickly. Too unassertive to discuss these incidents, he'd asked no questions. Now he saw there something was terribly wrong. Returning to New York, my father hastened with her to a physician. The diagnosis was juvenile diabetes.

That diagnosis tore my parents apart, marked them in a way that could never be fixed. For a brief while, they separated, returning to the safe harbor of their families. My father must have been decimated by yet another failure on his part. The plan of getting married had looked safe enough, even obtained the approval of the M.I.B.A. Philip and Kate were furious, believing that Louis and Minnie had put something over on them. "They must have known about her illness," Aunt Sylvia claims to this day. "Louis was a miser, but he was always running to doctors. He would have checked out something like that."

My mother was in her middle twenties, the time when juvenile diabetes often appears. She might have suspected she had the disease, or known it, and heeded her parents' advice to get married as quickly as possible. She lived in an age when physical defects made you "damaged goods," unmarriageable.

My parents decided to make a go of it, divorce being another "damaged goods" disgrace. Wounded, they limped back together, forming a truce, but the trust needed for a good marriage never developed. The Sonkins clung to the idea that the Paleys had betrayed them. My mother became the outsider.

When I try to picture my parents in those early years, I see two people circling, failing to achieve intimacy, their basic loyalties elsewhere. I see a dutiful daughter and son, each possessing family secrets. Only Clara knows when she really developed diabetes. Only Clara knows that Minnie, her mother, is suffering from breast cancer. Only Daniel knows how different he is from other people. Only Daniel knows the tyranny of his obsessive thoughts.

In time, my mother must have become privy to his anxieties, his sense of continually being out of place. Her friends, the ones he admired at first, made him uncomfortable. They were teachers, married mainly to doctors and lawyers. He compared himself unfavorably to the other husbands, even though my mother never did. The insecurity was in his head, planted there in childhood by environment, biology, or both. Clara accepted Daniel as he was; maybe that's what he found so disconcerting.

The years go by, and they're not good together, but they get used to being together, respecting each other's family loyalties. He agrees to move into the apartment building where Minnie and Louis live. She agrees to his spending time with his family without her. If he needs support, she knows he'll turn to his family. She'll turn to her friends or Minnie. Clara and Daniel are each too fragile to lean on one another.

Five years after the wedding, my mother becomes pregnant, determined to prove that diabetes has not made her "damaged goods." For the first time, everyone is united—Clara and Daniel, Kate and Philip, Louis and Minnie—in breathless anticipation. They disagree, of course, about who the child will be named for, an important matter in Eastern European Jewish culture. If it's a girl, my mother announces, the name will be Sara Jean, for Minnie's mother, Sarah Zishe, who had died two years before. The Sonkins are uncomfortable. They want the child named for someone in their family, and later on, they'll just call me "Jean," hoping to sweep away all evidence of that alien Sarah. In fact, I didn't learn my namesake until I started research for this book.

But the name is a minor problem. Basically, the families are on board for the first time since Kate and Philip had the brilliant idea of introducing Daniel to Louis's daughter. Or perhaps it was Louis who thought of introducing his marked daughter to Philip's rather unperceptive son.

Four months after my birth, Minnie's breast cancer metastasizes, and my mother's world crumbles, the bright hopes of motherhood turned to ash. She becomes a nurse to Minnie, and a middling sort of mother, turning over childcare to a live-in nanny. An early memory of mine is that she's gone off somewhere. I have the sensation of being lost, befuddled. Now I understand that my mother, too, was hunting—for ways to ease Minnie's final days. An all-consuming search, and perhaps my father, absorbed by his own self-doubt, provides little support. He helps by devoting himself to his daughter. For Sara Jean, he's always available, king of the sandcastles. With her, he finds the perfect respite from himself.

After Minnie's death, my mother's moorings loosen, yet she struggles onward. She brings her difficult father into the household because a dutiful Jewish daughter doesn't leave a parent on his own. Louis is a chill autumn wind, the odor of decaying leaves. He fills the medicine chest with leaking, sticky preparations, he parades around in long johns, he insists on a daily breakfast of shredded wheat and milk, for which he balks at contributing so much as a dime. Louis's presence undoubtedly ratchets up the tensions of the marriage. My father, unassertive as always, submits, but moves further into his shell. My mother is totally alone. Both are at emotional risk, but she's the one who cracks first. One summer, she suffers a "nervous breakdown" and is institutionalized for months. She comes home, pasted back together, and for a few years, everything is all right, that is to say, usual enough, from my point of view.

Then, in 1945, my father falls into the grip of a terrible obsession, the culmination, I deduce, of the guilt-producing thoughts that have plagued him all his life. This one is a super nova—the product of years of practice.

It had to do with the war, the draft, and the FBI.

In 1940, my father's draft board classified him 4F, exempt from military service, because of a shadow on his lungs that indicated an earlier case of unrecognized tuberculosis. Being exempt made my father think he was a slacker. He imagined that every customer who mailed a package to a serviceman was looking at him strangely. On the street, he steered clear of soldiers and sailors. "Why aren't you in uniform?" became the question he saw on every face.

When he went to work for the post office, he had lied about his age. He had only been sixteen, but he'd said he was eighteen. In 1940, to match his post office records, he told the draft board he was two years older than he was.

At some point in the war, with various adjustments in age requirements, the two-year age difference made him too old for the draft. Even though he was 4F, and not eligible in any case, he concluded he had committed a horrible crime in lying about his age.

Setting the record straight proved to be impossible. No matter how often he called his draft board, no one wanted to go through the bureaucratic hassle of making the change on the record. His request was irrelevant, given his draft status. The board's attitude increased my father's agitation. Why couldn't they see the seriousness of what he had done?

He enlisted the aid of his sister, Sylvia, who also worked for the post office. Her supervisor, a man with political connections, wrote to someone "high up" in Selective Service, but apparently, there was no fixing the records.

With each passing day, my father's guilt worsened, until a delusion was born. His crime was so terrible that the FBI would soon be coming to put him in jail. His arrest would bring disgrace on his parents, his wife, and his dear daughter. The only solution was to remove himself from the picture. He began to refer to his daughter as his "poor little orphan child."

He spent hours discussing this delusion with Sylvia, pacing the room, face flushed, refusing reassurance. He reviewed various methods of suicide and joked about the downside of each—iodine tasted terrible, knife wounds were messy, guns were too noisy, and so forth. His mind was a death trap, as dangerous as the theater of war.

My mother begged him to check into an institution, the one where she had received treatment years earlier, but he wouldn't agree. "Your father didn't like the smell at that place when he visited your mother," Sylvia told me. "And the food was terrible."

"Everything your family says is *Chinatown*," my husband once remarked, referring to the movie with Jack Nicholson and Faye Dunaway in which things make no sense. My father's talking about poison, knives, and guns, yet walking around the streets, because he doesn't like the food in a psychiatric institution. From the Sonkin point of view, it's a disgrace to be in a mental hospital. Better to suffer privately, within the family, where they can all suffer with him, and even maybe believe some of what he says, and no one else ever has to know.

My mother finds a psychiatrist who will give my father shock treatments in his office, and Sylvia takes him there. My father emerges dazed and bleary, but reaches into his pocket first thing for his draft card, which he cradles in his palm. "I don't care how much voltage they use," he says. "They'll never knock this out of my head."

Therapy with the psychiatrist goes no better. My father's main concern is not to upset the doctor. Since the man is quite tall, my father avoids mentioning anything having to do with height. The doctor tells him that he's suffering from a delusion. They need to explore the reasons why he thinks he deserves to be arrested by the FBI. He grows frantic at the doctor's inability to see the truth. "They'll never knock this out of my head." He relishes his role as self-torturer, flaying his skin inch by inch, preparing for the final ritual.

Despite his agony, he's the same as always with me, devoted, funny, loving—bending to my every whim—no sign of strain.

At least, that's what I remember, on the surface. But I remember below the surface, too, loud night-time arguments between my parents, my own fear, and shadowy images.

One morning, I thought I saw something. My father was shaving in our tiny bathroom; there was a dab of shaving cream on the mirror and one of Grandpa Louis' gangrenous medicine bottles on the edge of the sink. There was something funny next to the bottle, a gray object that frightened me. I stared, and the gray object disappeared into the folds of my father's robe.

Do I remember this, or was it a movie? Did I see my father, or George Raft?

I ask Aunt Sylvia, "Was there ever a gun?"

Yes, she replies. One day, she got a call from my father's co-worker. "He's got a gun in his mouth," the man said. The gun was U.S. government issue. Somehow his colleagues wrested it away, and the post office gave my father a leave of absence, not because he had filched their weapon, but because he was desperately ill. When co-workers wanted to find out how he was doing, they called his sister, not his wife, since his family was in charge, as always.

My father was a man who had stuffed a gun down his throat. He was busy obliterating himself, tearing up papers and photographs, giving clothes away—all signs of impending suicide. And still he remained at large, looking over his shoulder for the FBI, thinking there was only one solution.

And at the same time, he had to comfort me, his scary daughter. This was always my thought, how comforting he was, until I realized, later in life, that he had created the very terror he needed to assuage. The monster I feared in my closet was the illness destroying him; the dreaded conflagration, the ending he was about to accomplish: Soother-destroyer, dear father Vishnu.

Early one morning, as the sky casts first light, my father closes his copy of *Alice in Wonderland*, with its corner-off pages, and covers up his sleeping daughter. Then he silently leaves the apartment and races up the steps to the sixth floor. He has to race to keep going, to get beyond thinking. Cognition is a burning arrow aimed against the self. He longs for peace, yet, as he pushes open the iron door that leads to the roof, he's struck by the pain of loss. No more dear ones. No more *Alice* sessions with his daughter. Someone more deserving will read to her, he thinks, someone who isn't a criminal. He can't know that she will never be able to bear hearing *Alice in Wonderland* again.

He moves faster, stepping lightly across the corroded tar, until he reaches the roof edge, a low brick wall finished in brown tile. He hesitates, rubbing his fingers over the sandy texture of the edging. Surely he's been up here before, but always something has held him back, a lack of nerve, the hope of absolution. Today, he's ready; no, ready isn't the word for suicide—he's driven by a hundred Furies. Those evil witches are standing there, waiting—they lick at my father's feet, like the waves, they lift him up, over, and cast him downward. This isn't Rockaway Beach; he can't ride it out. He sinks to the earth, obedient to the laws of gravity, obedient as always.

He's alive and will be until an hour after he reaches the hospital. My mother comes, and I can't imagine what she does. Perhaps she says things she should have said years ago. Perhaps she holds him. Most likely, she simply waits and sobs until the police arrive.

For him, it's done, all those months of negotiating fruitlessly with the Furies. The harpies linger around the emergency room until he's ready, and then, transformed into fairy maidens, they carry him off to King Arthur's Avalon.

All that's left is my aching and the Sonkin family legend, the only way they can make sense of the illness that dogged him, the tragedy that claimed him: Daniel did the noble thing, he protected his family. He was too sensitive, too good for this world—a shining star, too precious to be the target of my anger, so I try to sidestep my feelings, but anger comes out in other ways, at myself, the world, and other people who have fathers. I wish my mother would remarry so that we could get him back. He must be out there somewhere, and she could find him again, if only she'd try.

A few months after my father's death, my mother, Louis, and I go to a small Catskills hotel where Louis knows the owners. One of the guests is a youngish man, slender and dark with balding hair. He makes funny jokes, and his eyes burn into me, as if he knows something about me. He attaches himself to us, and when he carries me on his shoulders, I can look down into his shiny baldness, the way I did with my father. I love him instantly, fawn on him. And then, suddenly, I'm ashamed, as if I've fallen in love with a shadow. This stranger can't fill up my emptiness—there is no other father out there for me.

As to my mother, the survivor, she seemed irrelevant, particularly when juxtaposed against my father's goodness. I was too young to think about what she might have needed or where she might be seeking it. I never saw her as vulnerable, at the mercy of unkind strangers, and I certainly never thought of my father as guilty of making her that way.

Never until I found my long-lost cousins, Anna and

Emily, and heard their accounts of my mother's "bad experiences." Then the ghost of Clara Paley Sonkin came to me, fifty-five years after her death, and she commanded my heart—mother, sister, and friend. I had to put myself in her shoes, not the teetering 1940s platforms I so admired on her sister-in-law, Theresa, but those sensible, brown oxfords she wore to school every day so she could stay on her feet.

I know that, for all these years, my mother's ghost has been suffering—the way ghosts do who have been raped, seduced, and left behind by their husbands. Her spirit feet are raw from prowling the netherworld, waiting for a daughter to appear and understand. My mother longs to sink down into the earth and rest, but she can't do that until her story is known, until she is vindicated.

And that's why I have to call my dear father to the court I've established in my basement, because now I'm standing in her shoes, stuck in them. I'm her defender and his prosecutor— two for the price of one, "daughter dearest."

Like all good prosecutors, I do my homework. I go to the Forty-second Street Library and look at the *Bronx Home News,* the local newspaper.

On May 20, 1945, I find a brief report of my father's death. "Injury in Fall Fatal to Man," reads the headline. "Daniel Sonkin, 38, jumped or fell from the roof of the six-story apartment house. According to police, Sonkin's wife, Clara, missed him in their apartment about 6 a.m. She discovered his body in the rear courtyard. Policeman Stewart, of the Bathgate Avenue Station, called an ambulance and removed Sonkin to Morrisania Hospital, where he was treated by Dr. Rose. He died an hour later."

This event, so pivotal in my life, exalted to an almost mythic level by my family, rated exactly four sentences of press attention. So the kind policeman's name was Stewart, and he called an ambulance. Did a siren sound? It must have, but for me there was only terrible silence, as if I had been sealed in a glass box.

Even the short shrift accorded to my father he has to share. On the same day, a woman a few blocks away also killed herself by jumping. Her name and my father's are paired, a leaping duo.

Reports of suicide in the *Home News* were almost a daily occurrence, so prosaic they rated scarcely a glance. Debt, disability, disaster, disgrace—these four horsemen lurked everywhere in those shakily middle-class streets, ready to send some poor bastard to the roof.

Many of the suicides, like my father's, bore the imprint of the war.

"Bronxite" Valentine Brandt, 59, a widower, hanged himself on May 22, after losing a son, a private at Camp Joyce Kilmer, to a hit-and-run driver sixteen months before. The war plant where Brandt worked had just closed down. Battered by losses, he had turned to the rope. Another case of "Man takes life."

Taking, taking, without end.

The obliterated self tosses its burden to others, like cargo falling off a truck in a skid, and the stuff lands somewhere, makes potholes somewhere—down the line.

Down the line is where I am.

A few days after the library visit, I again convene my basement court, but the basement goes out of control.

Suddenly, as I'm squinting in the dark, looking for my father, the whole place becomes as bright as day. There are floodlights all around, as if someone is being given the third-degree.

No, it's not an interrogation; it's a courtroom, box-like, depressing, but dispensing justice nonetheless.

There's a judge with a sour face and a pile of law books in front of him, and a row of men in double-breasted suits seated at a table. I deduce that they are the prosecutors. They invite me to join them. Strange that they have no papers, no evidence to introduce. Do I have to carry the burden of the whole thing?

The back of the small room is crowded with spectators, leaning forward in anticipation but resigned. They've seen many trials of this sort, and they are always the same. The prosecutors have no need of evidence because all that's required is a confession.

My father's ghost stands before us, strangely at ease, relieved to find people who actually want to hear about his guilt.

The situation is perplexing, though. My father's accusers don't appear to be from the FBI; they're too foreign looking, their suits too shiny and cheaply made. Still, a courtroom is where he always expected to find himself. Accommodating as always, he strains to figure out what they want.

The chief prosecutor, a fat man with a pencil-thin mustache way too small for his face, screams out the accusations. My father, he says, has betrayed the country, connived with capitalists, passed on government documents. His voice goes on and on; the spectators murmur in admiration, like aficionados at a bullfight. This guy is good.

My father's back stiffens as he starts to confess. "My guilt before the party and the country is great," he begins. A roar goes up from the crowd.

Suddenly, I understand what I've created—a court that doesn't distinguish between bullying and justice. I'm at a Stalinist show-trial, with a fix-up in advance verdict, intended to promote a political agenda, my own. I am the State here, judging without insight, condemning without mercy, just to assuage my own discontent with the way my childhood turned out.

Forgive me, I think, ashamed of my prosecutorial urges and overwhelmed with love for him.

I turn out the lights, and I banish them all—Eastern bloc suits, puffy faces, dumbed-down minds. Like Alice at the climax of her adventures in Wonderland, I hack the silly courtroom to pieces. "You're all a pack of cards," I cry.

"I knew you couldn't do it," a voice whispers. It's the psychiatrist. "There's that old Oedipal tie, you know, it never goes away." His voice is calm and oh so sure of itself—a man always in control.

And then I know how he captured my mother—by being the very opposite of my father, no trait in common except, perhaps, his Jewishness.

My seducer friend worships his own ego, even as my father worships his lack of one. He's a risk taker, fiercely competitive, thriving on criticism and spitting it back; my father hides from notice and becomes crushed by so much as a critical glance. The doctor is an empire builder in a world that favors the brave, my father a security seeker where there's no security to be found.

My father lives on guilt, but the seducer can't be made to feel guilty. He's full of self-esteem, entitling him to success, money, women. The authority of his profession makes his behavior impregnable. He dwells in a fortress, my father in hut of straw. My father could not have been other than he was.

But all those years of propping up the straw, holding it together, soothing it, must have made my fragile mother long for a shelter of brick. She bent to the strength of the psychiatrist, finding in him the "anti-Daniel." It wasn't a seduction; it was an antidote.

"Now you see," the doctor whispers.

The court is adjourned.

5
Two Sisters

CURIOUSER AND CURIOUSER. HOW comforting the information is that I've roused out of two cousins, I don't know. I've learned that my mother might have been raped, might have been seduced, and concluded that she might have been aborted. A bouquet of stinking flowers, yet they smell sweet, because they get me off the hook.

I always thought that my mother's death had something to do with me. Maybe I wasn't enough to fill up her life after my father died. Maybe she never really liked me very much; otherwise, she wouldn't have gone away, no matter how bad her diabetes got.

My relationship with my father was direct, with my mother ambiguous. Sometimes I loved her; sometimes I didn't, especially in that final year, when I blamed her for his not being there.

Once I even "acted out." I told her, "I'm going to run away." I didn't say "I'm going to run to him," but that's what I meant.

The courtyard of the building across the street had been converted into a victory garden. I crawled beneath the plants, tall as cornstalks, determined to wait until she felt bad. I scrunched down so low that the silken fringes of the plants brushed against my hair. From my hiding place, I could see my friends playing, but I didn't call out.

Hours seemed to go by. At length, the street grew quiet and dusk came on. I wondered if there were any animals that came out in the dark. I feared snakes, in particular, and someone had told me that about "Gardner snakes," small green things with a tendency to hang around victory gardens. I thought I could feel one crawling up my leg, but still I waited.

Finally, I peered out and saw my mother at the window of our apartment, surveying the street, a frightened look on her face. A wave of angry satisfaction swept over me but vanished quickly, replaced by sorrow and longing. I raced out of my hiding place, reaching our building so quickly that I didn't have time to brush the dirt from my clothing. It dropped off in clumps as I flew up the stairs, banged on the door, and fell into her arms.

Sorrow and longing have returned with the writing

of this book, along with something new, judging from the previous chapter—the fantasy of being her defender. Two conversations with my cousins, and I was off and running, dreaming up a lusty superintendent and an imperious doctor, sticking it to them, sticking it to my father, all because I don't like the way her life turned out. All because I don't like her having left me.

If I'd been older, wiser, the way I am now, I could have kept her around. That's why I need to be the defender. It's so emotionally satisfying to make myself useful to her. I realize that, if I use my imagination enough and keep time traveling, I can bring her back.

But fantasy isn't sufficient. If it were, I wouldn't be burning with the need for answers. I wouldn't be thinking about my mother's cousins, Emily and Anna. Are they telling the truth? Was my mother? I need a reality check.

One beautiful July day, I drive to the Poconos to visit Emily. I'm on eggs, like an adolescent preparing for a blind date. I check myself out—classic pants suit, good haircut, right amount of makeup, a pleasant-looking older woman, that's me. I'm determined to be witty, light, and outgoing. I want Emily to regret the years she didn't know me, when all she had to do was pick up the phone, and there's something else, too—I want her to spill all the beans she's got.

The soft glow of summer pervades the region, and proud purple flowers fight to be seen from the highway, overshadowed by commercialism—billboards, fast food restaurants, "kiddie" attractions. But a few miles off the highway is an almost perfect Norman Rockwell town only slightly down at the heels. I turn off the main street onto a winding country road that leads even further back into the nineteenth century.

Emily's farmhouse has no pretensions, unlike the restored jobs in decorating magazines; it's just a white wooden house a farmer once lived in, compact, tilting a bit, stabilized by a large red porch. The house stands on a rise, within hailing distance of neighboring farms but isolated from them. Emily is alone.

But not quite. The screen door flies open, and a huge mongrel dog, all legs and excitement, bounds onto the porch. "It's all right, Henry."

Henry's owner is a gray-haired woman of medium build with sharp features and a tentative smile. She's wearing jeans, a sweatshirt, and no makeup—a country woman. While shaking my hand firmly, she seizes Henry by the collar and directs him inside. Henry, though amiable enough, is a dog who doesn't respond to orders. He keeps pawing me and has to be placed in a cage that takes up almost a quarter of the dining room. Emily explains that she adopted Henry because he was an abused dog, and, though a fine companion, he remains unruly.

I sense she admires Henry's independence, which matches her own. It takes plenty of spirit for a seventy-seven-year-old woman to live here, tending a massive garden, struggling with a hyperactive pet, putting up with inconveniences, to have her life just the way she wants it. She tells me that, years ago, someone ransacked the house while she was out, a decimating experience, but she wouldn't think of leaving. "This landscape suits me," she says.

The inner landscape suits her, too—low ceilings, ancient walls, overflowing bookcases, a huge pile of wood, a kitchen that hasn't been altered since the 1950s. The most up-to-date items, and those that give her the most pride, are her grandchild's drawings, fastened by magnets to the refrigerator door.

Slowly, carefully—no help allowed, thank you— she prepares a luncheon of ham sandwiches on white bread, salad, and tea, which she pours from a cozy-covered pot. As Henry peers at us from his cage, she recounts her life from the time I last saw her as a perky SPAR.

The boy she loved was killed in the war. She married someone else, but the marriage ended in divorce. She's close to her two sons and her three granddaughters. She volunteers at the local library.

As to her childhood, she reviews the same story I heard previously—father's early death, mother's invalidism, the family's poverty, some kind of break with the relatives over more money, the kindness of Minnie and my mother in helping out whenever they could. I sense that my mother was a major player in this drama, a soother of wounds.

Emily confirms this. "Your mother was a very good person," she says.

I feel so comfortable that I neglect my major purpose, getting her to talk. Instead, I scrutinize, observing the way she slices the ham, pours the tea, considers the old family photos I brought for her to identify.

I'm looking for traces of my mother in Emily. My mother, too, loved the country, the Catskills, where she went to camp as a young adult. Is this country life something she might have chosen had she lived to be old? How cruel that she was cut off from me, my children, soft summer smells.

I remembered going to the park with my mother a few weeks before she went away. We stretched out on a greensward dotted with clover, the flower smell so juicy it stuck in your nostrils. My mother picked the fattest leaves of clover and wove them into a chain, which she placed around my neck, so I smelled like a flower, too.

She said Minnie had taught her how to make the chains. My mother showed me how to tie the stem of one flower around the head of another. You could make the chain marvelously long, long enough to twirl over your head, like a lasso. My playing Cowboy made her laugh, but even then, was she thinking of the superintendent and the psychiatrist? Had they been there yet? Were they ever really there?

Emily puts down the pictures I asked her to look at. She can identify only one person, Minnie's sister, Mollie, a major instigator, I surmise, of the family quarrel over money. "I'm sorry I can't be more helpful," Emily says.

"Actually, you can," I reply, mustering an everyday tone. "Was my mother pregnant? "

"It could be," Emily replies softly. "But you have to speak to my sister—she was closer to Clara."

We take Henry for a walk, or rather he walks us, sniffing his territory as he goes. Occasionally, Emily becomes breathless. Physically, she's not as capable as she thinks she is, or maybe that's what independence is all about. We go for a drive in her valiant old Mazda—worn carpeting, failing shock absorbers, stolid stick shift. Automatic, she tells me, isn't really driving. Vista after vista rolls by as Emily smiles contentedly. She thinks she is living in Paradise.

A few days later, I get a note written on the back of a grandchild's wiggled drawing: *Do call Anna; maybe she can answer more of your questions*, says Emily, directing me toward Delphi.

In the ancient world, when you went to see the Oracle, you had to be patient. If you weren't important enough to get an appointment right away, if you weren't Alexander the Great, for example, you might have to hang around for months, stoking the local tourist economy. Being likable increased your chances of getting pushed up on the list.

I resolve to ingratiate myself with Anna. I send her a printout of the Podonoff family tree based on data that she and Emily provided. A few weeks later, she returns corrections, noting that it would have been more "scientific" to make the chart horizontal rather than vertical. I gather that Anna, an academic, is a stickler for accuracy—a good thing, I reckon, for my quest. *Your mother was very dear to me*, she writes. *If you want information about anything, ask!*

I seize the opportunity. On the phone, I don't waste too much time getting to the point. "Was my mother pregnant?"

A long pause. "I don't think so," Anna replies, voice quivering. "I saw her shortly before she died, and there's no question that she did not look pregnant."

Her words are carefully chosen. Rapidly, she changes the subject, tells me about the continuing-care community where she lives. As our conversation ends, she exhorts me to "remember your mother as she was, a kind, intelligent, lovely human being. She was a thoroughly nice person. That's what's really important." In short, back off.

Anna is pushing a saint on me, but I need a real woman, the kind of woman who might even get "into trouble." "Nice person" simply isn't mother enough. "Nice person" is no one, and my mother must have been someone. Who? What could have happened to her?

If Anna won't tell me, I'll have to turn again to my imagination, my own *Alice in Wonderland* show.

Ring up the curtain: Stifling weather, sticky, sickly, 1946. My mother, pregnant and distraught, goes to the home of her brother, Bernie, and his wife, Theresa. It takes Theresa a few weeks to arrange for an abortion, but she gets the job done.

Afterwards, Theresa and Bernie go off on vacation, depositing my mother in Forest Hills to recover. My mother develops an infection. Terrified, Anna and Emily take her to the doctor, then summon Theresa and Bernie home. My mother is admitted to West Hill Sanitarium in Riverdale, where she dies five days later of septicemia, disguised on the death certificate as "diabetic acidosis."

The Sonkins, always there to pick up the shit when it falls, handle the funeral details. Grandpa Philip, cemetery chairman for the Minsker Independent Benevolent Association, keeps a log book so he can tell the cemetery which grave to open when a Minsker death occurs. Sometimes he makes mistakes, and occupied graves get opened. Families scream, Philip screams back, and his cemetery buddies struggle to make things right. But in the case of my mother, Philip doesn't need his book. The Sonkin family plot is where he'll bury Clara, right next to his son, Daniel. She'll be part of the family at last.

And there she lies, entombed along with the truth; indeed, the truth is buried more securely than she is, encased in a solid lead coffin, like the coffins the robber barons commissioned so their bodies couldn't be stolen and desecrated in payment for their many crimes.

I'll need a blowtorch to get at the truth. At the very least, I need some documentation.

I think about the sanitarium where my mother died, West Hill. It shut down in 1963, but the law requires medical records to be sent someplace. Of course, records don't have to be kept for fifty-five years, but perhaps my mother's was. Maybe it's buried in a solid lead file drawer, waiting for me.

A friend who writes on the history of psychiatry advises checking with New York Hospital-Cornell Medical Center, which maintains the archives of psychiatry. Cornell says the Archives have been transferred to the New York Academy of Medicine. At the Academy, I'm shifted from librarian to librarian. Finally, someone suggests contacting the New York State Department of Mental Health in Albany.

The woman who answers the phone confirms that the state keeps old hospital records. "But you have to speak to Jane," she says. "Jane knows all."

My heart leaps. But it turns out that Jane deals only with state institutions, not private places like West Hill. She transfers me to Rich.

Maybe he "knows all," too. Rich is a deliberate speaker, the kind of bureaucrat who gives his work careful consideration. I visualize him seated at a gray steel desk, surrounded by files, cross-referencing my strange request against the masses of information stored in his brain. He says he'll have to contact "the Alcohol and Abuse people," since West Hill treated addictions.

A week later, Rich calls back. There is a file, but it contains little, just an old ad for West Hill from a medical directory. A pause, as we both wonder what could come next. I can hear the wheels grinding, turning in his head. Finally, he says he's going to try to find out which hospital purchased West Hill. Would I please give him a ring next week?

When I do, Rich isn't available. He doesn't return my call either. A few days later, he's "in a meeting," the next week, "out of the office." I get the picture. He decided he's got better things to do than rustle up the ghost of a dead institution. How much of the taxpayer's money can I expect to have allotted to my quest?

But two months later, Rich calls. West Hill was sold to Regent Hospital, an upscale psychiatric facility in Manhattan. Regent itself is now closed, taken over by a mental health conglomerate.

"It's too bad about Regent and the records," he says. What? Well, a few years ago, there was an incident. Regent Hospital was dumping old patient records into garbage cans, right outside the hospital, where any passerby could pick them up and read confidential information. The newspapers got wind of it, apparently.

Rich can't imagine how his remark depresses me. I imagine a Manhattan garbage can, bulging with fetid newspapers, gum wrappers, scraps of clothing, oozing lunch bags, dribbling beer cans, goopy condoms—every disgusting thing I can think of—and there, at the very bottom, where you have to put your hand through all the crap to get at it, lies my mother's history, soon to be eaten by a voracious garbage truck. Before my eyes, the facts disappear—grind, crunch, grind, crunch. I see my project for what it is, a voyage through emotional garbage, a descent into the "mess" that marred my parents' lives—grind, crunch.

Rich's voice is so hypnotic, it's easy to slip into a trance, but I pull myself back. He's saying that not all of the Regent files were destroyed. Most went to the mental health conglomerate in California. He gives me the name of the person to call.

Lee Ann, the Director of Archival Retrieval, is warm and friendly. Hospitals are only required to keep records for twenty-five years, she says, so it's unlikely that my mother's record has survived. I have to send her copies of my mother's death certificate, my driver's license, and a letter stating that I want the entire psychiatric and medical record. The word "psychiatric," for legal reasons, is very important.

A few days later, I get a late-night call from Lee Ann. She's still in the office, having looked everywhere, but the West Hill files no longer exist. She sounds genuinely sad not to have better news, consoling, as if my mother had just died. "You know," she says, "even with a diabetic, it's highly unusual for a person to die of medical causes in a psychiatric institution."

Highly unusual—you bet.

I'm up against a wall, but I know there's a brick that will come loose, cause all the others to fall, if only I find the right brick.

Emily and Anna remain the best leads. My first cousin, Janet, the daughter of Bernie and Theresa, was a child my own age when my mother died. Not too likely that she would remember much, I tell myself, even though my mother was staying in the household. Besides, I have reasons for not seeking Janet so fast.

Keeping up contacts with the sisters, I discover a close, but rivalrous, relationship. Emily implies that Anna, who has a variety of physical ills, is a malingerer. "If only she'd get out and exercise a bit, she'd be okay." Anna thinks that Emily is too close to her sons and grandchildren. "She dotes on them." Anna's son, who lives in Canada, comes to the States but visits with Emily, not his mother. There's a note of triumph in Emily's voice as she tells me this. A hurricane races through the Poconos and damages part of Emily's house. "She should have had the roof fixed long ago," Anna sniffs. If one sister says "white," the other is likely to say "black." If one says "rapist," will the other say "psychiatrist"?

I write Anna that I'd like to visit, *not only to become acquainted, but to chat a bit about my mother. What you told me about her was unsettling but enlightening. Any further memories you can share, even if not totally positive in a conventional way, would be meaningful to me.*

"Well, you've laid down the gauntlet. She might not write again," says my husband. He glances at the piles of papers on my desk, all related to the search for my mother. He'd like to sweep them away, I know, because garbage picking has made me tense.

I feel a twinge of envy. *He* had a mother, a warm, supportive woman whom we both treasured. She died at the age of ninety-seven, her legacy to Solomon an inner security; my mother left persistent insecurity, a muddle that needs to be sorted out. I want more from her than I ever had, probably more than I'm entitled to.

"You hope I won't hear from Anna," I shoot at him. "You don't care if I never learn the truth."

"The truth," he says, "is us, our children and grandchildren—now."

My quest has left him feeling abandoned. I've wandered far away, down a rabbit hole, where he can't follow. I want support, but I'm not giving any.

A week later, Anna writes that she'd welcome a visit, requesting that we meet alone. Talking will be difficult, she says, but she wants to help me out. Solomon offers to come along, visit a museum, go to a shopping mall, but I don't want the pressure of his being kept waiting. I need time to time travel with Anna.

"I love you," I tell him as I drive down the Jersey Turnpike to Maryland, where Anna's continuing care community is located. All the way, my heart pounds. The roar of the traffic, distant because of my trance-like state, seems to confirm the promise of revelation.

Anna's section of the community consists of semi-detached dwellings called "cottages," in gray vinyl clapboard, much like the condos you see at ski resorts. Unlike

Emily, the residents have surrendered independence for ease and security—a communal dining room, rides to shopping centers, a medical facility, a nursing home should one be needed. Adaptive aging for the comfortable.

As I approach Anna's cottage, a whistling maintenance worker whirls about on a tractor, trimming the grass to perfect height. I get the feeling he performs this chore frequently, that nothing is allowed to get out of place.

Anna is almost a carbon copy of her sister—features broader, wrinkles more pronounced, eyeglasses thicker, figure larger. Like her sister, she dresses in no-nonsense fashion—chino pants, white T-shirt, sneakers, no makeup. No bra either. On one side of her chest, visible through the T-shirt, the outline of a pendulous breast; on the other side, the desert flatness of mastectomy. I'm reminded that she's my gene sister.

One eye focuses better than the other, but Anna peers intently, an eagle's gaze. "I didn't expect you to have gray hair," she says, made blunt by nervousness. Don't worry, I think, it's still little Sara Jean inside. Then she smiles, her dragon-like aspect evaporating. "I'm glad you came."

The "cottage" is standard upscale issue—white walls, cathedral ceiling, picture windows, contemporary kitchen, but Anna has personalized it with an impressive collection of books and art—arts and crafts pottery, Hudson River School paintings, Indian artifacts, and dreamy wooden structures painted in pastels that she created herself. In the bedroom, there are medieval works from France and Germany, seventeenth-century etchings, New Mexican *santos*.

The weather is disappointing, and the food isn't good, although people who don't know any better think that it is, and she had a more capable housekeeper before she moved to this community, but she acknowledges her need for care. Heart problems, high blood pressure, breathing, and balance difficulties—these have kept her from getting to the university library to do the work she adores, historical research. Her major companion is Lucy, an aged terrier, all docility, Henry's opposite.

I admire Anna's collections, the relics of a more vibrant life. Most were acquired with her husband, Hans, who's been dead for eighteen years. She shows me his picture, a tall, handsome man, with craggy Lincolnesque features and an air of affability. "He was good looking at every age," she remarks.

Hans is the only part of the past that Anna enjoys remembering. She asks why I brought along my mother's photos of the Podonoff family. I should have thrown them out.

We eat an informal lunch in the living room, paper plates balanced delicately on our laps, conversation just as cautious.

Anna recalls a summer when she was a child, staying with her mother at someone's home in the Catskills. My mother, who was at a young adult camp in the neighborhood, heard that Anna was bored to the bone. "She drove over to visit in a green coupe convertible. Oh yes, she had a car. Everywhere she walked, she seemed to bounce. All afternoon we joked and laughed. She cheered me up immeasurably."

So now I've gained a treasure—an image of my mother in a green coupe. I've learned that she could drive, had enough money to own a car, and was pretty independent. Most of all, I've learned that she could be happy.

Anna seems to guess my thoughts. "She was happy then, fun to be around. Later on, she was different, reserved, not the same person."

"Later on?"

Silence.

I ask, "I guess you mean after she married my father?"

Anna refuses to be direct. "He was a remote person, really, disinterested." She infers that she saw less of my mother after the marriage. "All I know is that I never felt comfortable around him."

It's hard to imagine that my father, so warm with me, so caring, could make other people uncomfortable. His insecurity poisoned the atmosphere, encapsulated him.

Why did they marry? I hear the words pouring out. I qualify the question. I mean, my parents were obviously so different. Perhaps it had something to do with my mother's diabetes. Does Anna remember when she contracted the disease?

In those days, people didn't talk about illnesses or the state of their marriages—and other people didn't ask, she says pointedly.

But I'm not "other people," or am I? I'm definitely an outsider in my mother's life.

I'm not surprised when Anna has little to add to what she told me on the phone about my mother's final days. Bernie and Theresa asked the sisters to take care of my mother for awhile. My mother told Anna she was having an affair with an important psychiatrist, and after a week, my mother left.

Where did she go?

"Home, I suppose," Anna says vaguely. She insists that she didn't ask my mother anything further about the psychiatrist and, no, she doesn't remember his name.

Pressing, I mention Aunt Sylvia's phone conversations with my mother. "She said she had an infection. You and Emily took her to a doctor, remember?"

"I never heard of anything like that," says Anna.

She shifts in her chair and changes the subject to Minnie.

When Anna graduated from high school, Minnie offered to pay for college if she'd agree to become a school teacher, like my mother, whom Minnie had also financed. Minnie had upwardly mobile ambitions and also, apparently, the ability to hide vast amounts from Louis.

In Yiddish, money salted away by a housewife is called a *knipple*, the word for handkerchief. Minnie was an expert in *knipple* management, Aunt Sylvia once told me. She financed the higher education of both her children, and she was willing to back Anna, too, but Anna was too proud to accept.

In her will, Minnie left Anna a generous sum. "I didn't know a thing about it until your mother came over with a check and said, 'This is for you.' There was a smile on her face."

The money came at a critical time. Anna had been ostracized by the family for planning to marry Hans, who was a refugee, not Jewish, and German to boot.

Apparently, the instigator was Louis. "Marry him, and I'll cut you out of my will," he threatened.

"I didn't know I was *in* your will," Anna shot back. The marriage became the center of a second family storm.

"Hans came from the German aristocracy and could trace his family back to William the Conqueror," Anna remarks. "When Louis attacked him, it was like a peasant downgrading a king—totally ludicrous." No accident that Anna's academic specialty is the British aristocracy, about as far from Louis and the Podonoffs as she could get. I recall the comment she scrawled on the family tree I sent: *Funny, but I don't feel as if I'm descended from these people.*

Several months previously, Emily had mailed me an old family photo she found of "these people." It had been taken in 1924, on the fiftieth anniversary of Sholem and Sarah Zishe.

Patriarch and matriarch sit surrounded by children and grandchildren, solemn Grant Wood figures in black, stunned either by the presence of the photographer or the strange trajectory of their lives. Anna and Emily, ages eight and four, are cross-legged on the floor, attired in matching velvet dresses. Emily remembered crying, frightened by the strangeness of Sholem's skull cap and his pungent body odor.

The photo tells the immigrant story: Sarah and Sholem, foreign, apart; their first-generation children, still bound by old world concerns (who can make money threats, who wields the power); and the grandchildren, jazz-age kiddos, my mother in a flapper dress way too large, Bernie, a bold, bored look on his face, the Arrow shirt man, and the little sisters, all dressed up with no place to go but out—far, far, away.

It took some emotional effort for Emily to dig up this picture. When I visited, she'd told me about it but said she didn't remember where it was. Like her sister, she had little interest in looking back, but for my sake, she'd rummaged through her drawers.

How much digging could I expect the aged sisters to do?

I put myself in their place. One day, out of the blue, they hear from a cousin they haven't seen for over fifty years. The call is such a shock, it temporarily loosens their tongues. Once again, they have to think about Clara in her doomed final days, Minnie, Louis, Bernie, and the little girl who was swallowed up by a "mess." Now the little girl is pestering them, but they're dried out, dead wood.

Anna looks straight at me. "I want you to know that, after your mother died, I worried about you a great deal. I was so concerned." Worried, concerned, but not enough to make contact.

I can see that the sisters needed all their energy for themselves. They put themselves through school, built marriages, cared for small children—their own children of the Howdy Doody Age whose mothers wore flared skirts with cinch belts and read Dr. Spock. The 1950s were out to bury the 1940s—goodbye to war worries, hello to prosperous peacetime. Easy to forget the past in the 1950s, even a mandate.

A time to turn away and heal the hurt of having a family that failed them. I got put aside, along with the rest of the Podonoff past. That was how they saved themselves.

Aunt Sylvia, almost Anna's age, could have done the same. When my mother died, Sylvia was a single woman with a steady boyfriend, but she included me in her future. Even as a child, I couldn't understand families in which this didn't happen. Grandma Kate had a sister, Ida, whose two grandchildren were in an orphanage. "Why can't Aunt Ida take care of them?" I asked. She was old, but so what? Kate was old, too. Oldness wasn't an excuse for not doing anything. For the Sonkins, there was never an excuse, because the past was present. Daniel lived through his daughter who was forever theirs. They had no need to "move on"; they didn't want to go anyplace Daniel couldn't go, too.

Like them, I'm a major practitioner of courting the dead. That's why this digging expedition doesn't seem odd to me, although I know it does to other people, Anna, Emily, and my husband, among them.

Anna stirs. "One lives one's life as well as possible, and it's not good to look back," she intones.

She sounds so pious, I feel like seizing her by the throat—but then she slumps slightly. She couldn't sleep last night, she says. Her blood pressure soared, and she developed a frightening headache. "I didn't expect this to happen," she says of the physical symptoms. Remembering, or trying not to remember, whichever one it was—my visit made her ill.

How could I have been so cruel?

Consumed with guilt—I don't want to commit murder, after all—I change the subject to Anna's work, and a completely different woman emerges, enthusiastic, involved. Without her professional self, the self she faced down Louis and the Podonoffs to create, Anna is a soul bereft. She describes an article a friend, a retired colleague, is preparing for an art history journal.

The article's subject is St. John Nepomuk, the patron saint of Bohemia, who is usually found only in European art. But Anna's friend recognized his iconography in several Southwest churches and also among the *santos*—small wooden statues of saints—made by local artisans. The craftsmen just called the figure "St. John," not knowing the difference between Nepomuk and the many other St. Johns. Why was this saint, so particular to Bohemia, popular in New Mexico? The friend traced him to the underground *penitente* cults. As she talks about academic matters, Anna's eyes glisten behind her thick glasses.

We continue the conversation over dinner in an upscale restaurant where Anna peruses the wine list with aplomb. We proceed from history to organized religion which, in her opinion, is only for the weak and superstitious. I knew my mother felt the same way, but I'm surprised to learn that Minnie did, too.

So the break with tradition began with Minnie; mother and daughter were in agreement, not conflict, as I had imagined, on such issues. Her guard down, Anna has dropped a valuable nugget of information, another treasure for my collection. The strong rationalism of the Podonoff women began with Minnie.

When I was a child, my mother wouldn't let me go to Sunday school with the other kids because religion was superstition. The taboo made me long to get inside the temple on Mount Eden Avenue, push open its great bronze doors. I loved stories and, from what I could see, the Jewish religion was full of them. What fascinating things might be hiding in this exotic building?

Later on, when I went to live with my grandparents, I was able to pursue my interest in Judaism. Anna seems to regard this interest as a betrayal of my mother, something foisted on me by the Sonkins. As for genealogy, another of my enthusiasms, it's appropriate only for people with bloodlines worth tracing, she says.

Annoyed, I regret having sent her the family tree but

not having created it. The Podonoffs, long missing from my life, have wormed their way in. If Anna wanted to sever all links, that's her business.

But all links are not gone. When we get back to the cottage, she asks, "Do you light Sabbath candles on Friday night?"

"Sometimes," I remark defensively. I think we're about to resume our spirited discussion when she heads for a bookshelf. There, behind the *santos,* is a pair of candlesticks. They belonged to her grandmother, my great-grandmother, Sarah Zishe, for whom I am named.

"I want you to have these," Anna says. The candlesticks are of the type made in Eastern Europe—heavy brass screwed into a hollow base, plain as all get out. Sarah Zishe must have brought the candlesticks with her, clung to them when she became a stranger in a strange land. There are tiny scratches on the rims where she scraped off old wax with a kitchen knife. Inside the holders, wax traces remain embalmed in hardened dust, like Miss Haversham's wedding cutlery. It's been five decades, at least, since a woman lit candles in these containers, shielded her eyes, murmured prayers, asked God's blessings on her children.

"If you polish them up, they'll look fine," Anna says, as if she'd held on to the candlesticks for their aesthetic value. But she knows they're not up to the standard of her collections. No fine art here, no British aristocracy. They're commonplace, Jewish to the core, her core and mine. She kept them because she wanted one memory of the put-it-behind-you *mishpocha*. Her secrets she cannot share, but this tiny bit of her heart she can.

I hug her, she laughs with pleasure, and we wrap the candlesticks in plastic bags.

I had planned to stay in a motel overnight, but I'm filled with longing for Solomon. Exhausted, I start the long drive home in heavy rain. I place the candlesticks upright on the passenger seat—two sentinels of the night. They bounce up and down in their ShopRite tarpaulins, murmuring a little *klezmer* song—"Sarah Zishe lit us, biddie-bum, biddie-bum, Minnie left us, biddie-by, biddie-by, Clara lumped us, biddie-bum, biddie-bum, Sara Jean loves us, biddie-by, biddie-by—hooray!"

"Pipe down you guys, I have to think."

I reflect that, though I have learned no secrets, I'm not disappointed. The sisters, with their cockamamie sense of independence, are fascinating. The more I know them, the more I know my mother, who sprang from the same complicated matrix. But was she like them or in juxtaposition—a dutiful daughter who followed the life plan her mother laid out—teaching degree, suitable Jewish husband (we could have done better, but there was that diabetes, remember)—or rebel who went her own way, as they did, but even further, taking a lover when it suited her? "You didn't know I was like that." Maybe she said it with pride.

Who was she really? Still the big secret, the one they refuse to divulge, because they want to protect her, even now.

Legend says that St. John Nepomuk was confessor to the queen of Bohemia. Her husband, King Wenceslas, was a jealous tyrant. He demanded of John the queen's secrets, but the holy man refused to break the sanctity of the confessional.

For this, John was martyred. The king's henchmen tied his heels to his head, gagged his mouth, bore him secretly through the streets, and cast him into the Moldau River. The story goes that, on the night of the murder, March 20, 1393, seven stars hovered over the water. In art, St. John is usually pictured with stars over his head and his index finger over his mouth, to show the value of keeping secrets. Anna's friend recognized him in the Southwest by this iconography, and that's how I now see Anna, lips sealed, steadfast, even if I were to truss her up and transport her to the nearest lake: keeper of the queen's secrets, high priestess of the hush-hush.

Never mind. There must be other ways of getting what I'm after, other traces of the queen's past. All the way home, I think about it and finally, I recall another place, a scary place, where I can look for my mother—if I dare.

6

Clara Sonkin, Deceased

"WHO KNOWS WHAT EVIL lurks in the hearts of men?" asked the 1940s radio program *The Shadow.* The Bronx County Courthouse, a building designed to strike fear into evil doers, has the answer. It's four blocks square, neoclassical, but grim as Alcatraz despite porticoes, friezes, and Doric columns. Enter this monolith, and you know you're going to get what's coming to you. Parthenon or purgatory? Only the innocent know for sure.

In 1946, when I was innocent, the building breathed fire. I was the dragon's prey, helpless while a battle raged.

The struggle began a few months after my mother died. I was settling in with my Sonkin family—Grandma Kate, Grandpa Philip, Aunt Sylvia, Uncle Robert—when a series of angry phone calls turned my grandmother wild with worry, crumpled handkerchief dabbing reddened eyes.

Uncle Bernie, my mother's brother, had decided he wanted to be my guardian instead of the Sonkins.

I liked Bernie well enough, and I enjoyed playing with his daughter, Janet, exactly my own age. Bernie's apartment was a glamorous place. His wife, Theresa, was like a movie star, dark and exotic with heavy makeup, smelly perfume, and heaps of Hollywood clothes in her closet. There were tight chiffon dresses with sequins, like the ones Carmen Miranda wore, rows of platform shoes high as the sky, drawers of tinkling jewelry, and Theresa didn't seem to mind if Janet and I rummaged through the stuff and dabbed perfume all over ourselves.

Theresa had marvelous talents. She could turn somersaults, stand on her head, and twist her slim body into amazing shapes, walking like a crab, bent over backwards. Theresa wasn't Jewish—even I could figure that out; she was Italian, a member of the "other" group that lived in our section of the Bronx. Theresa had been married before, a fact that wouldn't ordinarily be discussed with children, but she had an older daughter by her first marriage.

Carmella was a teenager and, in those days, I watched teenagers closely, imagining what the next phase of my life would be like. Carmella wore her hair in a pageboy, a style I thought would look good on me, and she was planning to be a "torch singer." Standing straight in saddle shoes, her mother's crystal necklace around her neck, she'd pretend she had a microphone and croon in the soft style of Connie Boswell. She was great, I thought, a star in the making, and I would be famous, too, because I was her cousin, or mostly her cousin.

Bernie and Theresa were fine for once in a while. But living with them would be out of the question. The feelings I had for the Sonkins were much deeper; we were connected at the roots, the way I'd been with my father.

A judge would have to decide who got me, a Surrogate's Court judge in the Bronx County Courthouse at 161st Street and the Grand Concourse, right near Joyce Kilmer Park, where Uncle Robert and I took long walks and talked about what I was reading. He'd given me my current favorite book, *Tales from Shakespeare*, by Mary and Charles Lamb, and I liked the stories so much we went to see a play by Shakespeare, even though I was only nine. Robert had been buying me books since I was a toddler and reading to me in his deep, sonorous voice, the voice of a speech professor, which was his job.

One of the first books he'd bought was *Babar*. He explained how the author had written the book in French, which was another language, but that book had been put into English, so we could understand it, and Uncle

Robert didn't stop explaining things to me except for the years when he was away fighting in World War II. With Uncle Bernie, there was no such closeness, so I didn't see why a court had to ask me where I wanted to be. All they had to do was call, but it wasn't done that way, apparently. There were papers to be filled out, and conferences with lawyers, and butterflies in the pit of my stomach.

Our lawyer, like every other professional in our lives, came through a Minsker connection. She was unusual in being a woman—and an opinionated woman to boot. There were two issues at stake, she explained: where I would live, and who would be responsible for administering the money my mother had left me.

At night, lying in bed, I could hear voices reviewing the case. "He's only interested in the money," Aunt Sylvia said. Apparently, Bernie couldn't take care of my money without having to take care of me. If I went to live with him, he wouldn't even like me very much. I couldn't imagine being without my grandmother's *challah*, my grandfather's jokes, Aunt Sylvia's word games, and Uncle Robert's walks. I didn't want to be a torch singer; I wanted to be with the Sonkins. I held on tight to the bedclothes. If a judge said I had to be with Bernie, I'd wrap myself in the sheet so tight they'd never get me out; even the police wouldn't be able to do it.

Ascending the courthouse steps, I clutched Aunt

Sylvia's hand, and I didn't let go inside. The courtroom was enormous, bigger than the Radio City Music Hall, where I often went with Grandpa Philip, an old vaudeville fan who loved stage shows.

But this was no show, even though the judge seemed to be high up on a stage, separated from the spectators by a huge railing. It worried me that the judge kept siding with Bernie's lawyer. He hated our lawyer, I could tell, because he frequently told her to keep quiet. That couldn't be good, but still she kept on talking in her loud Bronx voice, a voice my Uncle Robert would never have tolerated in one of his students in speech at City College. I had a sinking feeling in the pit of my stomach. Obviously, we had picked the wrong lawyer; we were going to lose, and I would have to twist myself to death in those bed sheets.

I didn't have to die. In a compromise, it was agreed that Robert and Bernie would be co-guardians and co-administrators, and that I would live with the Sonkins. The latter point was the only thing that mattered to me, but for Robert, working with Bernie promised to be burdensome. Bernie, like Grandpa Louis, was clever about money, while Robert, a college professor, had little experience with finance. In practical matters, he was sure to be bested by Bernie. At least, that was the view of Aunt Sylvia. "We lost," was the way she looked at the judge's decision.

I adopted this negative view, as I did many others, and I thought of the Bronx County Courthouse as a place where I had been done wrong. I didn't like to go near it—a major difficulty, since we lived close by. You had to pass the courthouse when you went to the Earl Movie Theater, or the Addie Vallins Ice Cream Parlor, or the Yankee Stadium. And your friends liked to run up the steps and hide behind the Doric columns, so naturally you had to go with them. But you weren't safe near that building, ever.

I didn't expect to find myself inside again, but in searching for my mother, I thought of the custody hearing. Perhaps there were traces of her in the court papers, a discussion of her wishes for me, maybe even how she died. It was a long shot, but worth a try.

One day I pick up the phone and call the record room of the Surrogate's Court. A friendly clerk urges me to "Just come on in and look at what we've got."

But it's not so easy to "just come in" to the Bronx County Courthouse. You have to walk through an electronic scanner, after first depositing your coins, keys, and other metallic items that could be mistaken for weapons into a small box. The boxes are constantly being shuffled by the guards and tossed about, so that the air rings with a tinkling sound and the Babel hum of voices—English,

Spanish, Haitian French, Chinese. On the line, there are men with swaggers, men with worried expressions, women with strollers, couples carrying lunch bags, children whiny or rambunctious depending on the degree of parental supervision.

The guards, in masterly fashion, direct people to the appropriate elevator banks for getting their lives sorted out—criminal charges, child support, custody issues, marriage licenses, death certificates—all can be resolved, if you know where to go.

At the Surrogate's Court, I'm handed a few strips of microfiche and directed to a room on the third floor where there are machines for reading the fiche.

The room, long and narrow, is crowded but not with fiche readers. Small groups are huddled in whispered conversation, defendants and families meeting with court-appointed attorneys for the first time, even though the case is on the docket today. The attorneys act as if there's a meter running, "plea bargain" the operative phrase. A child cries, "I don't want Daddy to go away." How many children has this dragon of a building devoured?

I squeeze my way to a machine, but the strip contains only an accounting of my expenses for spring 1949—Jack and Jill Children's Shop for camp clothes, Temple Adath Israel for Sunday School, Lynn Sofer for music lessons,

Alexander Sundel, D.D.S., for dental services. The list, dutifully prepared by Robert and signed by Bernie, testifies to the comfortable, vanished world of the middle-class Bronx, where Jews used to sit out on the Grand Concourse on summer nights, unhampered by fear of crime or the need for security checks.

But I'm not after nostalgia. I tell a clerk in the Surrogate's Court that I want the file for my custody hearing, not expense reports. "That's on micro*film*, not micro*fiche*," he says, and the bad news is that there's not a single microfilm machine in the building. I'm dumbfounded. "Well, the budget for the machines was cut," he explains, "and the law only requires us to have the stuff available on film, that's all."

"It's not really available if people can't read it," I shoot back.

He shrugs an *Alice in Wonderland* shrug. "Sorry."

I should have known nothing could go right for me in the Bronx County Courthouse. Damned if I'll ever go near the place again.

But then, a few months later, I run into a friend I haven't seen for a while and remember that she's an attorney in the Bronx Surrogate's Court. Katie, familiar with the logic of the place, smiles at my story of the orphaned microfilm. She tells me the public has the right to look at the original files, but old files get found more quickly if the request comes from the Surrogate's clerk, the job she holds. She'll borrow the file and Xerox the contents for me. I wonder if anyone will ask why the judge is interested in a sixty-year-old case, but, remembering the microfilm machines, I decide that questions are unlikely.

A few days later, a slim envelope appears on my porch containing copies of documents on "The Matter of the Guardianship of Sara Jean Sonkin." They include Bernie's petition to be my guardian, a waiver from Grandpa Louis assigning his custodial rights to Bernie, and the judge's decision appointing Bernie and Robert co-guardians. There are also various accountings, similar to the one I saw on the microfiche. Dull as dishwater, except for one document, which refers to "an air of hostility and a strained relationship between the co-guardians and their respective families." The hostility was so great that it took over two years to settle my mother's $20,000 estate.

Hostility. There it is—out in the open—the real nature of the feelings between the Paleys and the Sonkins, the real nature, perhaps, of my parents' marriage. How did this hostility play itself out in court?

To find out, I have to read another file, Katie says: the administrative file. That file turns out to be too fat for her to copy. "You better come in and read it yourself."

I drive to the Bronx with Katie on a late December day after a heavy snowfall. The Grand Concourse is silent, almost free of traffic, the way it was during the Great Blizzard of 1948, when my friends and I built giant snow forts and laughed with joy at having commandeered the entire thoroughfare. Inside the courthouse, serenity fades. I push through security with the mob while Katie whizzes ahead, flashing a badge.

When I catch up with her, she's set me up in an office that's used by several attorneys on a rotating basis, personalized only by a few children's drawings taped to the smudged walls. Law books in torn bindings are piled on bookshelves; an old phone book covered with fingerprints lies on the floor near wires where something was supposed to be attached. The computer, perched on the edge of the desk and not hooked up, looks out of date. Maybe the budget for computers was cut, too. In the rear of the office, glass doors lead to a snow-filled courtyard, near the doors a heating unit that clangs relentlessly, a familiar winter sound in Bronx apartments when I was growing up.

The room is overheated, yet I shiver. My file, *In the Matter of the Judicial Settlement of the Account of the Proceedings of Bernard T. Paley and Robert Sonkin, as Administrators of Clara Sonkin, Deceased,* lies on a coffee-stained desk blotter. Hands shaking, I loosen the serpent papers from their lair.

Clara Sonkin, Deceased, left an estate consisting of household furnishings, personal effects, savings accounts, a checking account, AT&T stock, United States bonds, and a teacher's pension. Bernard Paley, co-administrator, sold the household furnishings and personal effects for $475.00, he claimed.

Robert Sonkin, co-administrator, had problems with Bernie's accounting. Missing from the list of items sold, he said, were two fur coats, one mouton, the other Persian lamb. Bernie at first denied the coats existed. Later, he remembered them, but said they were included in the $475.00. Robert argued that the sum was too modest if the coats had been included, and too modest in any case, since my mother's high-quality furnishings should have commanded more money. His implication was that Bernie had stolen either the items or the money.

A more important issue was my mother's checking account. Robert demanded to see bank statements, check stubs, and vouchers, which Bernie was unable to provide. Bernie said he had seen these items at one point but didn't know what had become of them. Robert found it suspicious that Bernie would be so forgetful.

And then there was the mystery of the savings bonds.

Apparently, sometime before her death, Clara Sonkin had visited her brother-in-law, Robert Sonkin, and given him savings bonds to hold for "safekeeping." The bonds, currently in Robert's possession, were worth $2,300.00 according to Robert's calculations but $3,100.00 according to Bernie's. Bernie accused Robert of deliberately miscalculating.

The arguments drone on and on, with attorneys hurling charges.

Bernie's attorney says that Robert's attorney doesn't know how to write a legal brief. Robert's attorney says that Bernie's attorney is ripping off the estate in fees. As for the clients, they're entrenched, striking at each other with a vehemence born of long enmity.

I'm struck by the aggressiveness of my sedate Uncle Robert, the "unworldly" college professor. He's obsessive, in the Sonkin manner, determined to get his eyes on every document Bernie is trying to hide. Bernie attempts to beat him off with charges about the bonds, but Robert's a bulldog. After two years of non-agreement, the court, exasperated, appoints a special guardian to examine both parties.

Apparently, Robert has been waiting for this. With the guardian's permission, he hires an attorney who specializes in sorting out murky accounting. The expert orders copies of my mother's checking account statements for the two years prior to her death, the only time period available.

Painstakingly, the expert graphs the deposits and

checks them against my mother's known income, with surprising results. The graph shows that my mother ("the deceased") regularly made deposits substantially in excess of her income—unusual, indeed, for a schoolteacher to sock away almost twice as much as she earned.

Perhaps, the expert suggests, my mother had "an interest" in the men's clothing manufacturing business of her father, Louis Paley, a business in which her brother, Bernie Paley, is a partner. The expert questions the attorney for the family business, who responds: "Clara Paley Sonkin had no interest in her father's business or any other business that I know of. She received no money from the business. I never drew any instrument concerning any business or business venture for her."

I expect to see Bernie put on the hot seat about my mother's mysterious funds, but Robert draws back, apparently satisfied that, whatever happened, it didn't involve money being pilfered from the account. Shortly thereafter, Bernie admits that his attorneys miscalculated the value of the bonds; Robert's figures are correct. Mr. Expert advises Robert to drop the matter of the fur coats and accept the account of my mother's estate as amended. Bernie and Robert sign the account, and the case ends with Robert the victor. He's tracked down almost every last penny to which I'm entitled, and he's exposed what Bernie was trying desperately to hide—the slippery nature of my mother's checking account. Remembering Sylvia's statement, "He's only interested in the money," I amend it to "He's only interested in hiding something about the money." Bernie's no shark; he's scared.

Hiding seems to have been the family game, and my mother was in it, up to her eyeballs. But of her own volition? The more I learn, the greater the mysteries.

I can't help smiling when I think about the fur coats. I know what happened to them, even as Robert and the court did not. Thanks to my initial conversation with Anna, I know that Louis was trying to sell the fur coats before my mother's body was cold. Undoubtedly, he found buyers, and probably he sold other items in the apartment as well. He must have worked fast, in Louis fashion, and pocketed the cash before Bernie pointed out they'd have to make an accounting to the court, that the money was mine. But Louis wouldn't have understood such reasoning—any money he could grab was his; let Bernie figure out what to tell a court. Let Bernie take the heat.

Louis' ruthless avarice—the dominating theme of the Paley family—explains why my mother was wearing a mouton coat on the steamy July day when I last saw her.

I put myself in my mother's shoes, the shoes of Louis Paley's daughter, and I imagine that day.

Clara Sonkin gets out of bed in the morning and stares at her daughter, who is sleeping in the same room. Since Daniel's death a year ago, Sara Jean has been sleeping in his bed, her night terrors soothed by her mother's presence. Sara Jean can't know that, since the rape, Clara has been in terror, too. Last night, haunted by terrible dreams, she barely slept.

Glancing at her child, she heads for the bathroom, where she splashes her face with water and stares into the mirror. Her face is stone-cold white, like a hospital patient's, eyes underscored by enormous circles. The mirror is smooth, yet her image is fractured, savagely rearranged, a cubist painting of sorrow.

Barely aware of her father's raucous snoring, Clara stumbles to the kitchen, where she injects herself with insulin, puts on a pot of coffee, and then sits, slumped over the table, head in hands. Wherever she goes in this apartment, she can see the rapist's face and feel the touch of his hands. He's insinuated himself into the carpets, the draperies, even the cold metal of the kitchen utensils. He's hiding in the pictures on the wall, the Van Gogh reproduction she loves, and the Rembrandt etching. Wherever she goes in this apartment, she thinks of the psychiatrist and their affair, once comforting, now threatening, because of the pregnancy or the infection or whatever it is that troubles her. She needs to flee. Stay here, and she'll follow Daniel's path to the roof.

Clara calls her brother, Bernie, to come for her. She asks the Sonkins to come for Sara Jean. She tries to hide the humiliation in her voice at having to ask.

Returning to the bedroom, she packs a suitcase. Then she hides her most valuable rings, an opal and a wedding band, inside a pair of gloves. Four years later, Sara Jean, rummaging through the few items that were preserved for her, will try on the gloves and have the rings fall in her lap, like the gifts of that magic tree in Forest Hills.

By the time Sara Jean wakes up, Clara has everything ready. Despite the heat, she puts on the mouton coat. She wears the coat for the same reason she hid the rings and left a pile of savings bonds with Robert Sonkin some time ago. She knows she may be gone from the apartment for some time, perhaps forever. If she doesn't return, she knows her father will commandeer every item of value and try to sell it.

But even as she prepares to protect her possessions from him, she looks out for Louis. She makes sure he has plenty of food, the Shredded Wheat he always eats for breakfast, cans of chicken soup for dinner.

When Minnie died, Clara took Louis into her home, because that's what good daughters did. Minnie took in her parents, Sholem and Sarah Zishe, with Louis's acquiescence. Louis deserved the same, despite the fact that he was excruciating to Daniel, a wraithlike presence but her husband, nonetheless.

Perhaps Louis drives Clara mad, too, but that doesn't count. Since childhood, he's been omnipresent, his obsession with money a constant source of embarrassment. Minnie kept his tendencies under control, used her gentle manner to endow him with an air of civility while yielding to his whims. Every single night of their married life, she served chicken soup with poached chicken for dinner, as he commanded.

With Minnie's death, Louis is no longer the king. He's become wilder, more paranoid. Once he accused Sara Jean's playmate of having stolen his watch, which he later found buried under the newspaper. Clara had to go to the child's mother and apologize; Sara Jean was in tears.

For Clara, family has always been about Louis, working around and through him. Minnie showed Clara the working thing—how to accommodate, cajole, and quietly divest him of the cash he loved so much. Minnie was so good at it, she managed to establish her own bank account, and when Clara married, she too set up her own. Bank accounts make a woman free. So does keeping quiet about things, even to one's husband, *particularly* to one's husband.

Minnie and Clara were sisters of silence, but Bernie, the male child on whom Minnie doted, couldn't be quiet. He was rebellious, and after law school, which Minnie financed, he fled from home, eventually marrying Theresa, the colorful Italian contortionist. One can only imagine Louis's cries of rage. But Bernie couldn't maintain his independence. The Depression made one more Jewish lawyer superfluous, and Bernie was forced to join Louis in the business.

It's not difficult to figure out that Louis and Bernie don't get along. Why beat around the bush—they dislike each other intensely. Bernie complains to Clara of abuse, lack of proper remuneration. He has a family to support, a daughter the same age as Sara Jean, and a step-daughter. Louis treats him like a stable hand, calls him *goniff*—thief—when he tries to get what's coming to him.

When Minnie was alive, she mediated these animosities, kept up the illusion of peace in the family. Particularly, she looked out for Bernie, who had a heart condition dating back to childhood. Clara, having inherited this caring role, does her best. She uses her checking account as a vehicle for laundering monies Bernie "extracts" from the business, right from under Louis's eagle eye. She has no legal "interest" in the firm, but she is interested in straightening out inequities, as befits her social philosophy of fairness.

Perhaps she keeps part of the money for herself. After all, she has to live on a schoolteacher's salary, and Louis, though resident in the apartment, pays little toward expenses. It's a struggle to get him to contribute to the grocery bill. Clara keeps a notebook of expenses—so much for Shredded Wheat, so much for chicken soup—but she has to wheedle and shout before he puts his hand in his pocket and, after holding it there for several seconds, reluctantly pulls out some cash. These accounting sessions, which seem to go on endlessly, frighten Sara Jean, who covers her ears with her hands.

No, Clara reflects, it isn't wrong to redistribute the wealth. And Bernie is grateful. He and Theresa will care for her now that she's ill. But later, after her death, significant sums of "Bernie's money," buried in Clara's accounts, will slip beyond his grasp. Unless he's declared Sara Jean's guardian and administrator of her estate, prying Sonkin eyes will be looking into Clara's financial affairs. Louis himself may find out what's been going on. What a to-do Clara's death will cause for Bernie.

But right now, on this blistering summer morning, Clara Sonkin isn't planning on being dead. She hasn't changed her pension beneficiary from her father to her child; she hasn't made out a will or named a guardian for Sara Jean. She's in denial or in confusion, or maybe she's just plain careless.

Deciding on a guardian would be difficult. Much as Clara loves her brother, he's up to his ears in family responsibilities. Much as she dislikes the Sonkins, they are the people closest to Sara Jean. And, when it comes to money, she sometimes finds them trustworthy. That's why it seemed like a good idea to leave the bonds with Robert for "safekeeping," given Louis' proclivities. Clara can't know that Bernie and Robert will eventually lock horns over those bonds and everything else she has of value, including her daughter. She can't imagine the emotional distress she'll leave in her wake as she sails along, desperate for help, doomed to sink.

It's time to go. She holds her daughter in her arms, the fierce heat of the mouton coat stifling them both. Then she picks up her suitcase, weighed down with valuables, and, sinking deeper into the coat, she vanishes. Goodbye, you injured, lonely, loving, and mysterious lady, goodbye.

There now, I've put it all together, and it makes some sort of sense, doesn't it? I'm feeling proud, as if I could perform the same literary license on any set of legal documents, and heaven knows, there's no shortage of files similar to my own in the Bronx Surrogate's Court. I'm not only talking about the thousands filed or misfiled in the basement. Piled on Katie's desk, there are least twenty, families fighting over estates, making accusations, trying to tear children in two—legalese camouflaging greed, cupidity, anger. They should burn the files and force people to behave in a sane fashion. They should keep children from getting hurt.

Achhhhhhhh—I'm personalizing just a bit, and what's more, I have to go to the bathroom.

On the way to the ladies room, I get lost and find myself near a row of courtrooms. Peeking through a door, I notice that the room is not enormous as it seemed when I was a child. Why did it feel like the Coliseum, a lion waiting for me behind the judge's bench? Perhaps it's the intimidating décor, high ceiling, walls paneled in dark wood, the wooden balustrade with an enormous carved top rail. Yes, it's the rail that does the trick, separates the spectators from the action, reduces them to Lilliputians. How separate I was from the action, how ignorant, behind the rail.

The lights are off, but I imagine I can make out a figure standing in the front row. He beckons me, and I understand that I've simply moved my basement court to this official setting. I'm conjuring up a man I didn't know very well, my Uncle Bernie. During the custody hearing, I'd looked straight ahead, too frightened to even glance at Bernie. But I'm looking now, straight at him.

He's youthful, the way he was in my mother's old photographs—tall, athletic, blonde, with a confident stance, a facial expression that could be interpreted as knowing or haughty—the perfect picture of a 1920s football hero, lacking only a pigskin tucked under his arm and a leather helmet on his head. Bernie Paley—all-American. Like "Swede" Levov, the hero of Philip Roth's novel *American Pastoral*, he's a Jew who could easily pass for a gentile, nature's golden boy.

"Why are you doing this to me, Sara Jean?" he asks. "You don't even know me."

It's true. Of all my shadowy childhood figures, Bernie is the one I know least. I know even my mother better, and that's not saying much. My search is about getting to know her, and if Bernie has to be maligned a bit, so be it. But maybe I've colored things because of anger.

"You never called, and you were one of my guardians."

I know my words are less than fair. The file has made me realize how difficult it would have been for Bernie to contact me during two years of intense wrangling. Robert fought a great fight, acted like a knight in shining armor, but at the cost of my having a relationship with my mother's family.

"When it was all settled, well, then it was too late," Bernie says. "You were gone."

He sounds so distressed, I almost believe him.

"What I want you to know is about the money, how your mother got it."

I'm all inner ears, all invention. Then, to my horror, the conversation I imagine with the imaginary Bernie turns toward illicit activities.

"You were only a kid, but you must remember the war and rationing. I'll bet you couldn't even get any bubble gum."

I nod. Why is he talking to me as if I'm still nine years old?

"Well, it was tough for us clothing manufacturers to get by. The military took most of the textiles. Allotments were rationed, and even when we *did* get cloth, there weren't enough workers around to put the suits together. We could make more money selling our puny allotments on the black market than manufacturing."

He notices me shudder at the words "black market."

"Hey, don't be such a baby. That's the way it was. It's not as if we set out to do anything illegal. We'd be sitting there, wondering where our next buck was coming from, and then the phone would ring—a textile broker offering to buy our allotment. He's just around the corner, down the street; he can be over in two seconds. These were guys we'd been doing business with for years, guys your grandfather played pinochle with—Joe, Max, Sam. Who could say no? Certainly not Louis. And remember, we weren't the only ones—everyone was doing it."

Boring, boring—the oldest excuse in the world. I

won't give Bernie an inch. I stare at him, stone-faced, until he's compelled to keep on explaining.

"You're wondering if we worried about getting *caught?* Well, the government was carrying on an investigation, of course, but if anyone got nabbed, it was usually the broker. Still, you never knew when investigators might come poking around. The money had to be hidden. That's where your mother came in. If she didn't help out, she risked seeing her father and brother go to jail."

Bernie looks just a bit shamefaced. Louis made the arrangements, he says, and he had to go along.

His voice gets lower as he talks about my mother.

"She wasn't eager to get into it," he confides, but the words are a blur. Maybe he said, "She was eager to get into it."

Suddenly, Bernie turns sorrowful, blubbery, like those talk-show fathers who tell the children they've never seen, "I always loved you." I reach out my hand to touch him, but he floats away, sailing over the balustrade, finally disappearing behind the judge's desk.

After he's gone, I realize that he's the guy with all the answers—what my mother was like, whether there was a rape, an abortion, or an infection, why she died, whether she talked about me. I've missed my chance to pump him, used the time to make up things about him. Or have I imagined some truths?

I notice how deftly he put the blame on Louis, but he was Louis's partner—surely they were in cahoots, pressuring my mother. Or maybe she was their willing accomplice, looking out for father and brother the way she had all her life, and she put the money into U.S. bonds to assuage her conscience.

Of all my imaginings, this one frightens me the most, even more than the trial of the rapist and the psychiatrist. Allotment piracy was a bad thing. It drove up clothing prices and caused consumers to suffer.

But why am I saddling the Paleys with a crime? The courtroom atmosphere, for one thing, makes it easy to get an indictment. One leap, and I'm over the balustrade into the judge's seat, trying them in absentia for their real crime, which was—absence: absence in the second degree for Bernie, first degree for my mother. I hadn't realized I was so angry at her, so disappointed in him.

By the time I get back to the office I've been using, I'm sorry I started this mother search. Apparently, the only mother I wanted was the saintly victim, the humanist Anna urged on me. But the court file shows she was up to something not so saintly. I remind myself that human beings are multi-faceted, full of contradictions, and my mother had a perfect right to be that way, too. Still, she seems more ambiguous than most, forever inaccessible.

I feel like leaving, hanging out at the Greek coffee shop down the street until it's quitting time at the courthouse and I can hook up with Katie.

But the clank of the radiator urges me on. It's foolish not to look at the few papers left in the file. They contain an account of my mother's bills paid by the estate, thereby reducing the size of my inheritance. I can't guess that the statements will turn out to *be* an inheritance.

There are bills from the funeral home, the monument maker, West Hill Sanitarium, and also from a Dr. Aaron Wallace and a Dr. David Rosen, the latter for services rendered "to Mrs. Clara Sonkin, at the request of Dr. Paul Gordon."

In two seconds flat, I've struck gold. I never imagined I'd find my mother's lover or her abortionist (if either actually existed), but now there are intriguing possibilities. Dr. Wallace's bill was for $150.00, an enormous amount for medical services in those days, just about the cost of an abortion. Dr. Rosen's bill was for $50.00, the right amount for treating a serious infection, which was what my mother told Sylvia she had. As for Dr. Gordon, why would my mother need a referral to get an infection treated, when she had a family doctor? What was Gordon's specialty? What were the specialties of them all?

Almost five o'clock; just a few minutes left before I'm

scheduled to meet Katie. I dash to the Xerox machine and copy the most significant documents. I plunk down $15.00, twice what the job is worth, but I'm grateful to the Bronx Surrogate's Court for yielding up its secrets. Maybe they can put the money toward the purchase of a microfilm machine.

It's only a twenty-minute drive from the mayhem of the courthouse to the placid New Jersey town where Katie and I both dwell. We glide across the George Washington Bridge into serenity, but I'm carrying a mental briefcase of questions as heavy as the case Katie tossed on the back seat. It's a blessing to have information about my mother, troubling to find it hard to swallow. I'm in danger of regurgitation, the inevitable result of plying rocky waters.

But I know myself. I'm going to keep on sailing, and I'm going to steer clear of judgments. I remind myself that my mother suffered from depression, and that many things were beyond her control. You can't blame a person for mental difficulties. That's what she told me, and that's what I tell myself now.

7

Mental Illness Isn't Anyone's Fault

THE DAY SHE LEFT me wearing her mouton coat was the last time I lost my mother. The first time had been years earlier, at a left-wing summer camp in Massachusetts.

It was a camp for both children and adults. The kids slept in bunks, their parents, the grown-ups, in buildings that seemed terribly far away, perhaps as far as the Soviet Union, the country they all admired so much.

Sometimes we were at the lake, my mother wrapping a towel around me as I wriggled out of a wet suit. Sometimes we were walking through the meadow, looking for flowers. But lots of times, she didn't seem to be around at all. The whole experience was rather like the *Rugrats*, the adults disembodied voices, "the babies" on their own. And what a baby I was.

At night, I sank myself into an itchy blanket and sucked my thumb. The bunk was so cold, and the walls were so brown and the creaky floor was brown, too.

Behind the bunk, a few feet into the woods, there was a circle of stones surrounded by thick ferns. It looked like something in a picture book, and I believed it belonged to fairies. Sitting there, soothed by the odor of the ferns, I wished my mother would come to me. Wasn't that what fairies were for, to grant one's wishes?

A few years ago, I was talking with friends about sleep-away camps.

"I first went to camp when I was five," I remarked. "Maybe even four."

"Impossible," said a friend. "Sleep-aways didn't take five-year-olds. Maybe you were in Israel, on a kibbutz."

We all laughed, but afterwards, I dug out a picture taken on the bunk steps. My bunkmates and I have big bows perched on our heads, in the style of Soviet girls who hand flowers to Comrade Stalin, and we're wearing middy blouses and shorts. I'm sitting on the counselor's lap, a thin child with a wary, sad look. Anyone can see that I'm younger than the other girls by at least a year, maybe two. No wonder the other kids thought me childish.

I must have gotten in as a special favor to my mother. "Please, I need to have my child looked after," by anyone in shape to do it, which my mother clearly was not. What better place to get help than at a camp, for she had always loved camping.

I have photos of my mother at a Catskills camp in the 1920s, probably the same camp from which she visited to relieve Anna's boredom. My mother is the height of fashion—knickers and argyle sweaters, smashing shorts sets, woolen bathing suits like those worn by Florence Eldridge. *Camp Harmony*, reads a sign in one of the pictures.

Harmoniously, my mother and her friends perform acrobatics, joke about in canoes, make funny faces into the camera. Young men, several quite handsome, look at my mother with interest. True, her hips are a trifle large, but her figure's good enough, and her face is quite pretty—Ivory-scrubbed, exuding good nature. She looks joyful, a look that's unfamiliar to me.

Perhaps she was trying to capture the past by sending us both to camp. Perhaps there was no other child care arrangement she could manage.

In the middle of that summer, or maybe it was the summer after, things came unglued.

I was in the lake when a counselor beckoned, handed me a towel, and said, "Your mother wants to talk to you."

The counselor and I walked down the road, my towel dragging in the dust. Looming ahead, I saw an automobile. The door opened, and my mother stepped out wearing a dress instead of her usual shorts. Her face was flushed, and as she gathered me into her arms, her body burned. "I have to go away," she said. "I'm sick, and I'm going where I can get better."

Was that why she was so warm? If she had a fever, she could go to the infirmary; she could get better right here.

But looking at her grim face, I realized she wasn't going to do anything here. She was leaving.

"Clara, it's better fast," cried a voice from the car.

She ducked inside, the door slammed shut, and the car began to move.

Suddenly, there were torrential sounds, screams that seemed to be echoing back from the nearby hills, and they were coming from me.

I jumped on the dashboard, one hand clinging to a door handle, the other clawing at the window, searching frantically for her face. One foot slipped, but I hung on anyway. I lost a shoe, I lost my soul—just in the few seconds it took for the car to vanish. When I got back to the bunk, there was grass under my fingernails because I had cast myself on the ground after she left.

Emotionally, I was cold all the rest of that summer. No one spoke to me about my mother, but I was aware of sideways glances, underground murmurs. For the first time in my childhood, but not the last, I was "poor Sara

Jean," a little girl who had suffered a loss. Everyone hopes that nothing like that will ever happen to them. That's why they pity me. But I'm beyond them, here in my refrigerator.

When camp ended, my father picked me up at Grand Central Station and took me to the home of his parents, Grandma Katie and Grandpa Philip, the Sonkins. I lived with them and Aunt Sylvia, their then-unmarried daughter, for at least six months, one half of a school year. Uncle Robert was away in the war.

For me, there is safety in the order of my grandparents' lives. Unlike my mother, who has to race off to work in the morning, Grandma Katie isn't going anywhere. She's devoted to housekeeping, at which she's top notch, a *balabusta*, my grandfather says. She dusts, cleans, shops, irons, washes, cooks. She bakes—wonderful things, *challah* every Friday and strudel with thin dough you have to roll forever, stretching so thin it looks like Casper the Friendly Ghost's skin. I love the sure way she sprinkles flour on the enamel kitchen table, plops down the dough, and works it with a firm steady motion. I love the cracks in her hands and the way the dough sticks to them.

We go up to the roof, which has a fancy "roof garden"—tables and striped umbrellas, but also a macadamized section for hanging out the laundry. Each *balabusta* has her own clothesline. You wouldn't use someone else's unless she was a good friend, and then only when your line is sagging with overload. I pass the clothespins as my grandmother hangs each damp garment just so, because she has one way of doing everything, and it's the right way.

Avidly, we listen to radio soap operas or she recounts a plot when I get home from school. It takes my grandmother at least an hour to get through the details of a fifteen-minute program. She has to get inside the characters, say what they're thinking and feeling, and if they're crying themselves to sleep at night.

Sometimes she sings to me in Russian, that ultimate language of sorrow, "*Auchichornya* [Dark Eyes]," her favorite and, quickly, my own. "Dark Eyes," that's me, and her, and all of the Sonkins. My mother's different, though. Her eyes are blue. She's not *auchichornya* at all.

My Grandma Katie loves me, but for her, love and criticism are intermingled. She mourns the shortcomings of her children, including me. The trouble with me is that I leave my food on the plate, drop my clothing on the floor, play too loudly, swing too high on the swing. Her disappointments resonate, filling up that grand apartment, seeping into my soul. Whatever we do, we Sonkins, we're doing it wrong, but even so, we're together, secure in our love for one another.

One day, Grandpa Philip, a *bon vivant* whom I adore,

takes me to a movie starring Margaret O'Brien, the leading child movie actor of the 1940s. We're deep into the teary story when he tells me that Margaret can cry at the drop of a hat. "Why can't you be like Margaret O'Brien?" Philip asks. "She's the same age as you, but she makes a lot of money."

Here's something else I'm doing wrong. I don't have the slightest idea of how to get into the movies, much less cry on command. I feel terrible.

Maybe I felt that way because my mother was missing. She had a bad sickness, something to do with her mind. Aunt Sylvia told me she was in a hospital for mind fixing, a place with the word "West" in it. Decades later, when I learned from my mother's death certificate that she had died in a sanitarium called West Hill, I assumed that was where she'd been hospitalized earlier. Sylvia's memory had grown vague, but the name "West Hill" seemed right to her, too.

No one suggested that we visit or even call the West place. Perhaps children weren't allowed unless they were important, like Margaret O'Brien. Margaret would scrunch her nose, make her pigtails quiver, cry so hard the gates would open, and in she'd pop.

I clung to the fantasy of being Margaret finding her mother until, months later, my own mother reappeared with no explanation of her own. Our uneasy nuclear family—mother, father, Grandpa Louis, Sara Jean—was glued back together, but the experience made me wary of losing my mother again. I never worried about losing my father; we were bound together so tightly, he could never come loose. But I was wrong. A year or two after my mother's return, as I described in Chapter 4, it was my father who disappeared, jumping to his death from the roof of our building.

After the mourning period, my mother spoke to me frankly. "Your father died because he had a disease called mental illness," she said. "Mental illness is nothing to be ashamed of. It's like any other bad sickness. People who get cancer can't help it, and people who become mentally ill can't help it either. Mental illness isn't anybody's fault." I realized immediately that she was talking about herself as well. I didn't know then that, when she spoke of cancer, she had been referring to Minnie.

My mother explained that many people didn't understand about mental illness, so you could get stigmatized—treated unfairly—which I knew was a bad thing because she worked so hard in the Teachers Union to prevent unfairness. She told me I might encounter people who looked down on my father for having committed suicide, but he was just plain sick. Someday there would be a cure, and someday the public would be kinder. We had to work toward that day.

It made me feel less sad to have my mother talk to me like this.

A week or so later, our conversation served me in good stead. I was loading up my tray in the lunchroom when a classmate, a whiney girl who wore her handkerchief pinned to her blouse, whispered, "How could you stand to live with someone like your father?"

I slapped down my tray, grabbed her, and backed her into a corner. My voice shaking, I proffered my mother's "just like any other illness" explanation. Then, seized by feelings I hadn't expected, I pushed her, hard, into the wall. The "ping" sound of her head striking the tiles filled me with joy.

Terrified, she ran off.

"Let her be afraid," I gloated. "Let her think I'm like my father."

Standing up for him had made me feel powerful, and so did assisting my mother with her efforts.

My mother was active in a group working for the cause of mental health. It was also a support group of some kind. Sometimes she talked on the phone for a long time with people I didn't know. The group raised money and held meetings, parties, and dances. When I started to research this book, I tried to remember the name of the organization, but it eluded me.

I helped my mother with the fund-raising, knocking

on neighbors' doors, soliciting local businesses. It was tough, because mental illness wasn't like the March of Dimes or the Jewish National Fund with its blue box so familiar in our Bronx neighborhood. Even at stores where we were good customers, the shame-faced clerk would say, "Sorry."

Despite the buffeting, I felt our mission was terribly important. Time would vindicate us because we preached the truth—mental illness was a disease like any other.

One Saturday morning, my mother had an appointment with the president of a local bank. She emerged with an odd look on her face, took me by the arm, and ducked out the door. Bending down, she confided that the president had given her a check for a stunning sum.

"He told me his wife committed suicide," she said. "No one at the bank knows about it. He was in tears, because he can't talk, even to his family. Isn't that awful?" She looked as though she were going to cry herself. "There are so many secrets," she said, "so many."

I couldn't imagine then that, one day, I'd be probing her own secrets, plucking her from her grave, unable to say *kaddish* until I'd buried her on my own terms. Be patient, I tell her, it's for your own good. I'm coming to your rescue, like Margaret, all sobs and guts. And while we're on the subject of psychiatry, Mother dear, I'm hunting for your doctor-lover, a prominent butt on which to pin the blame for what happened to you. Psychiatrists are a part of the mental illness picture, too. Maybe going to bed with them isn't anyone's fault.

From the file in the Bronx Surrogate's Court, I had the names of three doctors—Aaron Wallace, David Rosen, and Paul Gordon, the last of whom had referred my mother to Rosen. What a windfall. I savored the names with angry satisfaction. Soon business would be booming at my McCarthyesque bar of justice.

From an old medical directory, I learned that Aaron Wallace and Paul Gordon were psychiatrists, David Rosen, an internist. Gordon and Rosen had offices in the same building on the Grand Concourse; probably they had a professional relationship that would allow Gordon to refer my mother for a discreet abortion. But Rosen was a pillar of respectability, director of medicine at one noted Bronx hospital and a senior medical board member at another. Would he risk all that on an abortion?

My mother might have consulted Rosen for other reasons. Perhaps he treated her for the ill effects of someone else's abortion, or for an infection caused by rape, or for some other kind of infection, the run-of-the-mill kind that menaced diabetics and carried them off.

Rosen wasn't really in my sights. Wallace and Gordon, the psychiatrists, interested me more, since both fit Anna's description of my mother's lover as "an important man." Researching them, I discovered that Wallace was one of the early figures in the group psychotherapy movement, Gordon the president of a neurological society. Both were advocates of outpatient electroshock therapy, and they cited one another other in articles on the subject. Clearly they were colleagues. Neither mentioned having lost an office patient to suicide, but Wallace also matched Aunt Sylvia's description of the doctor who treated my father—a shock of thick gray hair, tall and imposing, so tall he had to lean over when he shook Sylvia's hand.

Amazingly, both had backgrounds similar to the lover/doctor I had imagined—Jewish, of Eastern European birth, trained in classic psychoanalysis.

Of the two, Wallace was by far the more prominent. In the late 1920s, he founded Westmount Hospital up in Westchester. Today, the hospital has been absorbed by a major medical center and it still provides premier psychiatric treatment.

Wallace was an activist, a messiah, the leader of the movement against stigma. He taught that mental illness was a sickness like any other and not anyone's fault. He urged his patients to stand up for themselves and fight prejudice. Don't hide the fact that you've been sick, he said; use your experience to help other people.

Former patients heeded the call. They founded the Wallace League to raise money for Westmount, spread the truth about mental illness, and support discharged patients. They found out who needed help and hastened to provide it. You couldn't leave Westmount without being enfolded in their fervent arms.

The New York Academy of Medicine Library has a single issue of the newsletter they published, dated in the early 1940s. There are folksy news items—come and visit the club house, be sure to get your tickets for the annual dance, there'll be a conga line and lessons in rumba dancing—interspersed with searing stories of illness and recovery. In a plea to relatives, a former patient expounds the Wallace philosophy: "Your son is now mentally ill. You hide the fact. You feel ashamed. Eventually you will learn that, in this day and age, the mentally ill, with the aid of medical science, get well as often as the physically ill. Your son's stay at Westmount can be made much more pleasant if you cooperate with him—by becoming more familiar with mental hygiene and learning to understand that there is no stigma in ever having been mentally ill."

The library's card catalog notes that the name of the newsletter's publisher, the Wallace League, was eventually changed to the League for Mental Health.

Reading the words, I have to steady myself. Memories come flooding back—newsletters on my mother's desk, the pamphlets we pressed on resistant contributors, all bore that name—League for Mental Health. A name I heard almost every day, somehow it got ploughed under, along with my mother, in my private slash-and-burn operation.

I understand at once that my mother had a treatment relationship with Aaron Wallace of many years standing. Probably it dated back to her first hospitalization, after she left me in camp, at a place that must have been Westmount Hospital, not West Hill. She was a Wallace follower, a proselytizer of his beliefs, and it was to Wallace that she turned for help in the final weeks of her life—weeks that, judging from the size of his bill, must have been desperate.

I need to know Aaron Wallace and his work, for, in the treatment he provided to patients, I can find my mother. In his articles, she may be disguised by a pseudonym, but I'll recognize a scrap, and I'll be content. I don't know if Wallace was her lover as well as her doctor. I don't know if, at her behest, he tried to save her desperately ill husband, but I do know that he played a significant role in her life.

Surely the major medical center that absorbed his hospital must house the archives of Aaron Wallace. But the center's librarian hasn't heard of Wallace or his papers. "He was important in the history of psychiatry," I remark, appalled to find him so completely forgotten.

I shouldn't be. It's more than four decades since Aaron Wallace died, almost seven decades since my mother fled to his sanctuary, but for me, time is moving backwards. I expect others to be where I am, in the 1940s, on my mother's trail. If this continues, I'll soon be in need of Dr. Wallace's treatment myself.

The librarian says I'm welcome to read back issues of the *Journal of Westmount Hospital.* An anniversary issue undoubtedly has information about Wallace. "Just let us know when you're coming."

I find the worn journals in stacks stuffed into a hallway near the men's room. One contains a history of the hospital.

In the 1920s, a mental health society asked Wallace to found an "experiment"—a hospital for the "borderline mentally ill"—neurotics and others who weren't functioning but who would not normally be hospitalized. Admission would be open to all, regardless of race; rates would be low, and free to those who couldn't pay. All of these provisions were unique at the time for a private institution.

Wallace planned to feature group therapy, a relatively new form of treatment. In groups, people were more open and honest, he believed. The group was the best place to gain insight.

In a Westchester village, Wallace found the perfect property, the decaying estate of a bankrupt millionaire. With the aid of wealthy board members, the mental health society renovated the place and renamed it "Westmount" because of the winding curve leading up to the main building. The rise was a "mount" only by Westchester standards, but the name, a joke at first, took hold. Wallace insisted on calling Westmount a "hospital" rather than an "institution" because he intended to produce cures, as with any other disease. Later, his designation would turn out to have legal implications.

Isolated from the village, Westmount was like a commune, with few distinctions between patients and staff. In Wallace's view, work was therapeutically valuable, so patients painted buildings, rolled tennis courts, raised vegetables, repaired furniture, waited on tables. Working together, staff and patients cleared the weeds from a saltwater pond and created a fishing hole. They built a lopsided recreation hall. In the evenings, there were parties and musicals arranged by the patients, warm, happy times.

Wallace saw Westmount as a therapeutic Utopia, a kibbutz of kindred souls, some ill, some healers, all devoted to cure.

The town didn't share his vision. Plenty of townsfolk called Westmount "the nuthouse" and spread sinister tales—patients hanging themselves in the woods, a nurse fighting off a cackling attacker, an old man who chased neighborhood children.

In the late 1920s, the zoning board turned down Westmount's plans to expand. On appeal, a state supreme court found that Westmount was an "insane asylum," not a hospital, as Wallace maintained, and therefore that the zoning decision was "reasonable, not oppressive, and constitutional." The mental health society fought all the way to the U.S. Supreme Court, which dismissed the case, citing no federal interest. During the six years of legal wrangling, hundreds of townspeople signed petitions, later filed with the court, calling the expansion a "menace."

Reading about these events in an historical society newsletter, my blood boils. How I'd like to get my hands on those worthy citizens—the people who need to have attitudes adjusted, their heads pushed against the lunchroom wall. I'm back in grade school, punching out justice for my father. I'm walking beside my mother, inflicting League of Mental Health pamphlets on the disinterested, because that's her legacy. She wasn't around to teach me much, but she taught me that stigma stinks.

The stench burned in Aaron Wallace's nostrils, but

he prevailed. His "experiment" flourished and achieved a national reputation—so nah-nah to you, benighted burghers of Westchester.

Wallace was often asked to describe the Westmount experience. What happened there to make patients better? The answer, he said, lay in the political structure of his establishment, a structure that was certain to appeal to people, like my mother, with egalitarian views. In the following paragraph, I've altered his words, but only slightly, to fit my mother's case:

Imagine a woman who has been suffering emotionally for many years, unable to meet the demands, either real or imagined, that are made on her. Finally, she finds the situation unendurable; her functioning grinds to a halt; she can't tend to her little girl, go to her job, or endure the presence of her husband. She consults a psychiatrist, who advises hospitalization. His words are like a "seal of doom," a confirmation of her inferiority. She fights the idea, yet she needs an affordable sanctuary where she can be nurtured and healed. Eventually, she is *healed—by Westmount's close-knit democratic society. Here, distinctions fall away, all are equal and supportive of one another. The factory worker and the schoolteacher become bosom friends.*

There must have been hundreds of schoolteachers treated at Westmount, yet somehow I think Wallace is writing about my mother. And I seem to remember a woman who could have been the factory worker.

I met her at a League event she hosted, a children's

party, I think, in a section of Manhattan I'd never visited before—Hell's Kitchen. To get there, my mother and I had to walk through an alley filled with garbage cans and climb several flights of smelly stairs. My mother explained that not all apartment buildings had elevators, a fact that had never occurred to me.

Inside the apartment, there were children racing about and adults seated on threadbare furniture. The sparseness of the place frightened me, although its owner was friendly enough.

She was a painfully slim woman with unkempt hair and several cracked teeth, not my idea of what a mother should look like, but my mother seemed to like her a lot. The two of them chatted on the couch in an intimate fashion, hands clasped together. I played uneasily with the other children, longing for release from an environment I found alien.

Still, I was glad to be admitted to my mother's world, a world my friends would never get to see. For the most part, their mothers were housewives, home to greet them after school but deadly dull and asking too many questions—"Why aren't you wearing your rubbers? . . . Did you eat all your lunch?"

My mother didn't care about things like that. She cared about what was happening in the world; she cared about eliminating stigma. And clearly, she cared about the crack-toothed woman who, I now realize, must have been a pal from Westmount.

The get-togethers sponsored by the League for Mental Health were a continuation of those at Westmount itself. Wallace arranged for picnics and other family events to encourage children to visit. He wanted them to learn there was nothing to fear from a mental hospital. But I never visited, and I never learned. To me, my mother had vanished into a dark pit. She was lost, and I was locked out.

But not any more: I've read many of Dr. Wallace's articles, so I can imagine what being his patient must have been like. I can smell the country air at Westmount. I'm on my way in Margaret O'Brien mode, a child/woman whose movie star status grants her admission. I wave my pigtails and the world salutes. Scottie, beam me down.

I imagine a summer day in the early 1940s. I'm standing by the rec center, which tilts a bit because it was constructed by amateurs. Inside, someone is playing "Chopsticks" on the piano. Suddenly, the pianist switches to "I'll See You Again." I feel encouraged—a message. Here at Westmount, I can find my mother.

Up the path, I spot the main building, half Victorian gingerbread, half Greek Classical Revival, appropriately odd. The entrance, I figure, must be off the porch.

I trot along, past patients playing tennis; others, seated on Adirondack chairs, stare glumly into space, a dead giveaway that this is no resort. But the atmosphere is almost congenial. To one side of the path, two white-coated orderlies joke with a patient.

Entering the building, I see a blonde woman seated in one of the living rooms. She's wearing blue shorts, a white T-shirt, and the same multi-colored sandals she often wore to the lake at camp—the camp where her daughter is wondering what became of her. My mother is getting ready for her first group psychotherapy session; we're both getting ready, but I have an edge. I've brushed up on the techniques of Dr. Aaron Wallace.

We walk down the hall to a small room where eight women are seated in a circle. Dr. Wallace believes the ideal group size is six to eight. Margaret O'Brien makes nine—odd woman out, little girl out.

The doctor is so tall that his legs extend far into the circle, but his most notable feature is his piercing, kindly eyes. His manner is relaxed, yet energetic—he's prepared to stir things up. For the group to work, he has to jump in, feet first, as member, not master. Group therapy, he believes, should be egalitarian.

Wallace begins this session, as usual, by talking about some aspect of psychoanalysis. Today, the subject is repression—how we can force our minds to forget unpleasant things. But clamping down can result in psychological symptoms. "We can't close ourselves off," he says.

The group hangs on his words as on a life raft, but my mother shifts her legs uneasily back and forth. What will be expected of her here? She notes with relief that Dr. Wallace, after introducing her to the group, appears to have forgotten about her.

The first patient to contribute is Betty T., a shy young woman seriously depressed since the birth of her first child a few months ago. She's afraid of the infant. "She doesn't seem real, more like a doll," Betty says tearfully.

"Maybe you're worried that you're going to break her—you know, hurt her," another woman pipes in. "I felt like that with my first one."

Dr. Wallace says that children aren't really fragile; they're actually pretty tough and, in time, parents learn how to take care of them. "Perhaps you need to have more confidence in yourself," he suggests. Betty may also have aggressive feelings toward the baby, so she sees her as breakable. Two group members nod in agreement, and one says she knows how difficult it is to admit such feelings. Betty smiles uneasily.

Suddenly, Wallace fixes his eyes on my mother. "Well, Clara," he cajoles, "tell us about yourself."

I learn forward. Yes, yes, Clara, do tell.

My mother, so reserved by nature, feels as if she's

under a spotlight. Seeking to avoid exposure, she provides only the bare essentials—she's a schoolteacher married to a postal worker, and she has a little girl. Her father, a widower, lives with the family. Her problem is that, lately, she's been unable to do anything at all. It's an effort to move, like carrying around a pile of rocks. She feels crushed and helpless.

Wallace smiles sympathetically and says she won't always feel that way.

He looks around at his patients. No matter what the symptoms, he believes their troubles stem from something that went wrong, way back when, in the original group—the family. By the family, they were criticized, rejected, discarded. All human beings need to belong, but his patients never had that need fulfilled. Here, in the group, a new family is created, one that will love and accept them. Feeling secure, they can learn to understand themselves. Feeling loved, they can give up the immature behaviors that are making them ill.

By the group, they were traumatized; by the group, they can be saved.

This is Wallace's deepest belief. Although Westmount offers other forms of treatment—individual therapy, insulin therapy, hydrotherapy, electric shock—group therapy is a central focus. It takes time, he says, four to six months at least, for group sessions to accomplish their purpose.

I sit there through the warm fall and early winter, like a mother waiting for her child to get used to nursery school. "Come-on, Clara, get mature," I murmur, not remembering anything particularly immature about her, except perhaps her leaving me. But then, I don't remember much about her at all.

Of course, it's the 1940s, and there is no air conditioning. Worse still, there are no anti-depressants, no Prozac, no relief from the darkness. I think about how difficult it must be for my mother and the others in a time without these drugs. I think about how dead they will be by the turn of the century, the century in which I'm writing this book. Then it will all be pointless—the anxiety, acting out, repression, trauma formation, consciousness, yearning for acceptance, to say nothing of the struggle to get well, the fierce concentration it took to liberate one's brain without drugs. Liberating took so long, so long ago.

I think of James Joyce's brilliant story "The Dead," which ends with "snow falling faintly through the universe and faintly falling, like the descent of their last end, upon all the living and the dead." Rest in peace, says Joyce, you who are here and you who have departed.

But I can't let them rest. It matters terribly to me to resurrect this group, to relive those months when Clara

Paley Sonkin at last opened up, because ultimately, I imagine she did. She was trying to tell me something, and if I breathe the air of Westmount long enough, I imagine I can hear her. I imagine I hear these revelations and the group chiming in:

September: "I get so annoyed with my husband at times—he doesn't seem to be listening to me. He's in his own world. Sometimes I think he's only comfortable with his family. I wish he would spend as much time with me as he does with his mother."

Mabel W., a widow in her late fifties, says that, when she finally stood up to her dominating mother-in-law, her husband got angry. Mabel discovered that he cared more for his family than he did for her. Maybe this is what Clara's afraid of finding out.

Dr. Wallace thanks Mabel; her suggestion is a possibility. But no matter how Clara's husband behaves, she's a desirable person. Her husband might not feel good enough about himself to give her the love she needs. But that's his problem, not hers. Clara gives it some thought.

October: "I feel as if I'm stuck between my father and my brother. They're always fighting, mainly about money, and it makes me sick to my stomach, as if I was responsible somehow. No matter what I do, I can't keep them from going at one another like savages."

At this, Betty T., the young woman suffering from

postpartum depression, begins to cry. Her parents fought violently, she says, and she always felt responsible for their divorce. It's the first time she's mentioned the divorce in the group.

Dr. Wallace points out that divorce is a "breaking up"— maybe that's why Betty sees her own baby as breakable. She's projecting the guilt feelings she had about the divorce onto her infant, undermining her ability to function as a competent mother.

Guilt probably plays a role with Clara, too. The antagonism between her brother and father goes back many years. In their struggle, both managed to take center stage, diverting their mother's attention from Clara. Guilt feelings can be a cover for anger, the doctor suggests gently. He asks Clara if her mother favored her brother. At first she shakes her head but, then, reluctantly says, "Yes." She looks down at the floor. It's all right to express her anger here, someone says. That's what the group is for. They've all been through it.

November: Weeks ago, Clara told the group that becoming a mother was a thrilling experience. Now she wonders if she ever wanted a child. Perhaps she only wanted to please her mother, who did not have many years to live. Clara weeps as she says this.

Betty T., who is starting to recover, says she was overwhelmed by negative emotions about her child. She's come to understand that women don't feel the way they're "supposed to" all the time. Maybe it's all right to doubt you ever wanted to be a mother. Dr. Wallace says Clara needs to give herself permission to have "unacceptable" feelings. It's okay to be ambivalent, even hostile, if one understands where the emotions are coming from. Clara nods but continues to cry. Betty T. puts her arms around her.

I wish that I could play the comforting role I've assigned to Betty T., but I'm bound by the odd time-warp arrangement I cooked up myself. My mother's salvation will have to come from the capable hands of Dr. Wallace.

Wallace's view is that his patients are emotionally needy and, like infants, unable to bear frustration. Maturity—a synonym for mental health—lies in learning to be realistic. In the newsletter of the Wallace League, a patient writes, *We are taught that, in a case where we cannot get what we want, we should try to accept a substitute.*"

Find a substitute seems to be the Wallace prescription for life's disappointments.

In an article about group dynamics, he writes about an unemployed, middle-aged stock salesman who aspired to move in circles that were "socially and financially above his reach." After the group pointed out the salesman's limitations, thereby teaching him reality, the man decided to seek a lower status job, a "substitute" for the sort he really wanted.

Accepting substitutes means, basically, accepting one's circumstances. But some circumstances are truly drastic, like those of Mr. H., married twelve years to a nagging harridan. Since being married, H. had developed anxiety symptoms, particularly while headed home from work. In the group, he first insisted he was happily married, but after gaining insight from another patient's experiences, he admitted he wished his wife would "croak."

Wallace doesn't say what "substitutes" Mr. H. accepted in order to stay in this marriage from hell, but it's a good bet he wasn't encouraged by therapy to leave. In the 1940s, divorce was shameful and, also, a mark of immaturity. The 1960s, the decade that made self-actualization a national mania, had not yet arrived. Instead of fleeing rotten relationships, patients were taught to find a way to expect less or emphasize other aspects of their lives.

This is the therapeutic philosophy that Dr. Wallace would have employed with my mother. He might have analyzed her case thus:

"Mrs. S. is the second-generation daughter of Eastern European Jewish immigrants—a demanding, self-involved father, and a compliant, striving mother. Mother favored older brother, suffering from heart disease since childhood. Patient resented attention to brother but sublimated these feelings into becoming "the good daughter," mediating angry relationship between brother and father. She's intelligent, ambitious, but uncertain whether the decision to become a schoolteacher was her own or her mother's.

"Patient developed diabetes in her early twenties. Neurotically refused to accept limitations of the disease. Determined to become wife and mother, she married an introverted man overly attached to family of origin, who was unaware of her condition. She feels unable to reach him emotionally.

"Patient traumatized by mother's death, which she sees as a failure on her part. Has ambivalence toward her child, guilt about husband, repressed anger toward father and brother. This is a woman driven by feelings she doesn't acknowledge and needs that cannot be fulfilled as she demands." In short, the patient is having reality problems.

I imagine Dr. Wallace's individual therapy with my mother. He tells her that she wanted all of her mother's attention but couldn't get it. Her father was too demanding, her brother too ill. To get love, she became her mother's assistant, doing good but repressing anger. Her diabetes made her, at last, the center of attention, but in a negative way, tarnishing her "goodness" as a daughter.

Rather than accepting a more limited life, she persisted in getting married and having a child. Her antagonism toward her husband is based, in part, on not having been honest with him during the courtship period. She's also angry because he won't provide the emotional closeness she needs.

Dr. Wallace assures my mother, "Clara, you are a lovable person. It's just that Daniel cannot give to you as you would like. He has difficulties, but these are his, not yours. You need to accept his limitations and your own. You cannot make things right between your father and your brother. You cannot change your father's character or your husband's. If you can't get what you want, try to substitute. Seek emotional satisfaction in your work, your wide circle of friends, the causes that interest you. Wanting what you cannot have is making you ill. In facing reality, you'll find a cure."

Aaron Wallace imparts all this in the most empathetic way, his brown eyes brimming with concern. Despite his height, he's a gentle man, a father figure, with a personality that's almost hypnotic. Some patients, it is said, get well just by sitting with him.

Well, that's where I'm sitting, with him and my mother—listening. And I'm falling for him. Why not? His sense of confidence is comforting, not abrasive, like the egomaniacal physician I imagined in Chapter 3.

There's no doubt my mother is under his spell. For

years to come, he will be the authority figure in her life, the savior she seeks in times of crisis.

They're very close, but were they close enough to "wind up" in his bed, to use my mother's words to Anna? Maybe Wallace needed a "substitute," too.

If there *was* a psychiatrist/lover, Wallace could fit the bill. But it breaks my heart to think about this affair precisely because she needed it so badly. To be swept up, valued, cared for—at least to have the semblance of these things—my mother deserved all that, but not the accompanying pain.

It's troubling to think the affair might have been of long standing, dating back to her hospitalization at Westmount. If so, my father could have known about it. It might have increased his feelings of inferiority, contributed to his illness, an agony for him and a terrible burden for my mother. "You didn't think I was like that, did you?"

Most likely, though, the affair, if there was one, began after my father's death, perhaps after the rape, if there was one, when she turned to Wallace for solace.

And now, I'm full force in the middle of this therapeutic romance. I hear phone calls in the night, whispers. I wonder about the times she isn't home at night, leaving me with Grandpa Louis, supposedly at meetings. I wonder where they meet, the empathetic doctor and the vulnerable widow. Or does every tryst occur in his fine Manhattan office?

If he *was* my mother's lover, Aaron Wallace was truly a hypocrite, ignoring not only ethics but the rules of the "group family" he created. An affair with a patient would be tantamount to emotional incest, making a mockery of his beliefs.

But such hypocrisy would not be unusual in the history of psychiatry. Carl Jung is said to have made mistresses of at least two of his patients, and Otto Rank had an affair with the French writer Anäis Nin, who was his patient.

I prefer to think that, if there was an affair, Wallace wasn't like these "giants," driven by narcissism, but the victim of counter-transference—the feelings summoned up in the therapist by the patient. He may have been lured by a fantasy, common among shrinks, of rescuing a damsel in distress. My mother was that, all right; she had problems enough for two damsels, maybe three or four.

I can't be harsh on Wallace. The man's history proves his worthiness, and I'm impressed by the devotion of his former patients.

Ah me, I've run out of blame, but not out of theories.

I remind myself that there was another psychiatrist in the picture—Paul Gordon, a Wallace colleague.

Gordon was an editor of the Westmount journal and

also a Westmount consulting neurologist, referring patients to the institution. He may have referred my mother to Westmount, or perhaps it was Wallace who referred my mother to Gordon for follow-up after she left the hospital. That would have made sense; Gordon's Bronx office was quite near her home.

Gordon might well have been the psychiatrist/lover, if there was one. The affair made my mother feel so guilty she fell into a depression and turned to Wallace for help. Things happened in the wake of the affair—infection or pregnancy, a need for my mother to be treated by Gordon's colleague, Dr. David Rosen. Another possibility: An affair with Wallace led to infection or pregnancy, a need for my mother to turn to Gordon and then be treated by Gordon's colleague, Dr. David Rosen. And somewhere in the crowded picture, a rape that might have been responsible for infection or pregnancy, a need for my mother to be treated by Gordon's obliging colleague, Dr. David Rosen.

Enough of this. I get into my car and drive to the building on the Grand Concourse that housed the offices of Rosen and Gordon. My appointment is long overdue.

Solomon agrees to come along. I tell him I'm afraid of getting lost, but that's not the real reason I need his company. I know the Grand Concourse like the back of my hand. What I fear is knowing it too well, the floodgates of familiarity, my first sight of the building where "it" happened, whatever I take "it" to be. I'm afraid of whatever lingers, yet I pursue.

Today's Grand Concourse is so different from the sedate boulevard on which I grew up. The street is bustling with people, yet even on a sunny day, everything seems dark because of the deteriorated housing stock—boarded-up windows, missing bricks, brass balustrades replaced by wooden poles, the menacing effects of graffiti.

To say the place has lost its class would be an understatement, but class—or was it pretentiousness—is no longer the issue. Now we're talking about survival. Now the standard is an apartment minimally free of vermin, a row of strong locks on the door, an elevator that works most of the time, a superintendent who looks out for the tenants, a lid on drug dealers. On all these counts, the Concourse rates higher than surrounding streets. That's why it's still grand, still mine. Even the Puerto Rican flags plastered on buildings can't convince me otherwise.

I dart down the street, Solomon close behind, ducking women with baby carriages, construction workers with ladders, old men gossiping, young men loitering—"bums," the Jews would have called those young men, but not to their faces, not then, not now.

The building I'm seeking turns out to be something

extraordinary, a ten-story gray brick replica of Manhattan's Flatiron building right in the middle of the Bronx. From a distance, it looks like a flagship, free as the wind, but drawing near, I see that it's imprisoned by metal scaffolding. The metal scaffolding, topped by torn blue plastic, obscures the ground-level apartments below. Green bars cover the windows of these hidden residences, making them look like jail cells or a mad monastery. There's so much metal, the building appears to have no door, a sure signal, I think, to wrap it up and walk away. Then I spot a man pushing on some glass with vertical green bars on either side.

The glass swings open; Solomon and I squeeze in behind him. We come face to face with a barrier, a metal security door. The man buzzes himself in and holds the door for us—some security. In two steps, we're flat up against the battered door of the elevator. A family emerges, laughing and joking, snaking around all obstacles to the street.

This lobby was always small due to the building's flatiron design, but now it's truncated, claustrophobic. All charms have been, of necessity, undone—the entry foyer butchered by the security door, a cozy alcove transformed into a laundry room, the once-tiled floor painted crimson red, the kind of red used for basements.

And what of those "medical suites," which legitimate

the pride of a Concourse building through its specialists, "important doctors" in residence?

I look around in bewilderment, but it's Solomon who finds them. Right off the "laundry room," there's a door with a piece of paper reading *Supt.* Across the lobby, another door with a multitude of locks. These two residences were once the swell medical offices of P. Gordon, psychiatry/neurology, and D. Rosen, internal medicine, so close that the doctors must have bumped into each other coming and going. In this lobby they chatted, compared schedules, arranged to meet for lunch. In nearby Jewish delis, now replaced by luncheonettes serving *cuchifritos,* they discussed cases—including, no doubt, the case of Clara Sonkin.

And in one of these two medical suites, some treatment was given to that patient, that woman, that mother of mine.

I stand transfixed, staring at the two doors. From beneath, I see a substance oozing; it's red, like the floor; green, like the bars on the windows; black, like the grave—play dough of the soul that I knead to my own meaning. I twist it into the infection my mother suffered, the placenta she may have lost, the vaginal material, suffused with guilt, that she expelled in the arms of her lover. The stuff continues, serpentine, around the perimeter of the lobby, undulating to the rhythm of the machines in the laundry room—a mad dance of despair and decay.

The thing heaves about—red, green, black, or is it black, green, red—twisting and oozing, gobbling and regurgitating, spreading out over the floor. It catches on to my heels, holding me fast. I rarely get dizzy, but I'm dizzy now.

Solomon grabs my arm. That's why he came, to pick me up, even before I fall, because there are no doctors in this building, not anymore. Before I know it, we're back in the car, headed down Jerome Avenue toward the Expressway.

I wonder if the tortured, twisting, turning thing I imagined I saw wasn't really my mother, striving to adapt to reality, accept her circumstances, follow the Wallace prescription. She adapted and adapted, and then something tipped the balance and she couldn't adapt any more.

Oh, Dr. Wallace, it buried her, all this adapting. Can't you find her a camp where the trees are in bloom and friends are canoeing on the lake, and there's a big wide lawn filled with flowers? And this is my wish: She would want to have her little girl with her, and they would not raise money or do anything good for mankind but just be together, making chains out of clover—wouldn't that fit the bill, doctor? I think so.

8

Waiting For Moskoff

MY MOTHER HAD A "substitute interest," to use Dr. Wallace's words—the Teachers Union of the City of New York. The union was more than a substitute, it was a passion, a love affair with a renegade, for the union had a troubled history.

In 1940, the Rapp-Coudert Committee, a committee of the New York State legislature, investigated the union for communist influence. In 1941, the American Federation of Labor expelled it because of communist influence. In 1948, the CIO, which had welcomed the teachers after their split with its rival, threw them out for basically the same reason.

In the 1950s, all hell broke loose. The New York City Board of Education interrogated hundreds of teachers suspected of subversion. Fifty teachers were fired; 250

more resigned or retired. The system cleansed itself of the best and the brightest, the cream of the crop, because these were the people the union attracted. In the wake of the investigation, there were suicides, lost livelihoods, familial dissension, betrayals—the common sequel of witch hunts.

The price of loving the union was high, but the union offered a lot in return—a heady sense of changing the world. Though it never represented more than a tenth of the city's teachers, it went beyond the usual demands—better pay, better benefits, smaller classes, job security—and onto the promise of righting social wrongs.

In the 1940s, the intellectual inferiority of poor and black students was a given, segregation the norm, even in New York City. Black children were educated in deteriorated, overcrowded buildings, assigned to "remediation" and "retardation" classes in wildly disproportionate numbers.

The union called for an end to IQ-testing. It exposed anti-minority bias in textbooks. It demanded better facilities in Harlem and Bedford Stuyvesant, more black teachers, an intercultural curriculum and, finally, integration—all this at a time when the word "integration" was scarcely a whisper.

Full and total equality—this was the goal for all children, all people, everywhere.

Being a teacher was exhilarating because the future rested on what you did in your humble classroom. Each day you could bring the new messiah—social justice—one step closer. Many of the union members were Jewish women, like my mother, and many had exchanged traditional religion for political activism, but the messianic fervor was the same. For these women, the union was a cause, a comfort, a home—a second-generation *landsmanschaft* of people who hailed from the same emotional territory, the immigrant Jewish family.

They were "the school-teacher daughter," carrying the family's expectations of advancement while seeking to embrace the brave new world of left-wing philosophies. They were "modern" yet tied by duty to a past that threatened to weigh them down. Inevitably, they experienced internal conflicts. But whatever a woman's problems, she knew that other teachers would find them familiar. In the union, she had a natural support group, and, on the political level, she was an eagle, poised to alter history.

Changing the world required social action—rallies, protests, and petitions, particularly petitions.

On the desk in our living room, beneath the bust my mother had sculpted of her mother, Minnie, there always rested a pile of petitions, long sheets of drooping paper. What they were for, I don't recall, but I looked on them as something potent.

In the second grade, I sat next to a boy named Philip, who was a special friend. He was funny, lively, and mischievous, and he couldn't keep from popping out of his seat. Nowadays, Philip might be diagnosed as suffering from attention deficit disorder; then he was merely "naughty."

Once a year, a professional troupe of children's actors performed at the school. This show was much anticipated, and Philip and I talked about how much fun it was going to be.

A week or so before the event, the teacher announced that Philip, because of his behavior, was not going to be permitted to attend. I've never forgotten the crestfallen look on his face. I walked home puzzling over what to do. Philip was being punished for something he couldn't help, a clear case of injustice.

Injustice was handled by petitions. I took one down from the desk. That evening, my mother helped me write out a statement that we, the undersigned members of Class 2A, requested that Philip be allowed to go to the annual show. I enlisted the aid of some friends, and we worked quietly, shepherding classmates, one by one, into the clothes closet and having them sign. No one refused, though we often had to explain what a petition was all about. I felt privileged to have this wonderful knowledge.

A short time after we handed in the petition, the teacher said that Philip would be going to the show—a triumph for social activism. I enjoyed that performance more than anything. Philip even stayed in his seat. (As I write this, it occurs to me that the teacher was probably a union member herself.)

When I set out to "find" my mother, I remembered the petitions, her activism, and the union. I realized that, in the union, I might locate her spiritual shadow, if not the woman herself. And I had an idea of where I might find the union.

Long ago, a friend, my co-author on another book, set out to write about the teacher witch trials of the 1950s. Under the newly passed Freedom of Information Act, she sued the New York City Board of Education and obtained transcripts of teacher interviews, board memos, and other materials relating to the firings. Then she doggedly tracked down as many investigated teachers as she could find, and interviewed them all, both martyrs and informants.

For various reasons, Linda never wrote the book, which was to focus on the issue of communism and the union. I remembered that there was a stack of cartons gathering dust in her garage. One winter afternoon, we piled them into my car. "It all seems so long ago," she murmured, looking at the cartons fondly. Talking to these people, she had empathized with their passion, bemoaned their fate, idealized their cause—in short, fallen in love—and then, as publisher after publisher failed to do likewise, finally laid the teachers to rest.

Now I proposed to open the tomb. "I'll get the stuff back to you soon," I promised.

"No hurry," she said, and looked away.

Reading Linda's material is like venturing to Shangri-La, finding a tribe of beings, pure, untouched, naïve. They are, in the words of one teacher, "attracted mainly to things outside themselves." The truth is that they live for things "outside of themselves." Their identity is not just "teacher," but "union teacher," as if they belonged to a special kind of order. Without the union. . .well, it's impossible to imagine the world without the union.

A quarter of a century after the dismissals, talking from the kitchen of a Bronx co-op apartment, the back porch of a Berkshires cottage, or someplace even further away from their roots, the comments are always the same—the union was a high point.

"It was inspiring."

"The finest people I ever met and ever knew."

"The most wonderful years of my life."

And the work was so important. We were the best teachers, the key players, needed by the children, trusted by the parents. "In every school, parents depended upon the Teachers Union members for knowledge, information, and ideas for how to help the schools."

We were soldiers on the barricades, the barricades we built ourselves. "What did we use to do?" a man asked Linda. "Well, we would go to certain schools in Harlem and Brownsville and hand out leaflets saying things like, 'Dear parents, if you go to Room 327, you will see the ceiling is falling down on your children every day. If you go here, you will find such and such.' Well, that's dirty politics. They hated our guts for that."

"They" were a melange of characters to be opposed—the reactionary bureaucracy at the Board of Education, crazed anti-Semitic principals, and non-union teachers who dispensed bias. In Linda's files, a 1949 letter from a parent complains of a Mrs. Fletcher, assigned to a school in Brooklyn. Fletcher tells the children that "Italians are born beggars." She berates Jewish mothers for "sending their children to Hebrew School too much." For every group, she demonstrates contempt.

The union won't stand for this kind of thing. The union makes noise, brings down the ceiling on the Mrs. Fletchers.

And, in the 1950s, "they," the gut haters, get even. The world turns black, unrecognizable; here, in the safest of professions, things are suddenly unsafe. Friends disappear or, even worse, turn on you.

"Everybody with the least bit of leftist leaning was considered a red," recalled one union leader. "And the reds, of course, were the most awful things in the world. Even people who normally were decent were so terrified that they'd lose their job. People suddenly found themselves in positions where they had to appear before a committee and say that they saw so- and-so at such-and-such a meeting, whether it was so or not, or else they would lose their jobs. When you have a wife and kids, you just don't want to—it's a terrible feeling. When I lost my job, all my friends in the school retired from the union. They resigned *en masse*. Of the whole group with whom I was friendly, not one person sent me a note, not one person came to see me. It wasn't that they didn't want to, don't think they didn't."

The first victim of the terror, the first of 334 teachers to be interrogated, was little Minnie Gutride, a forty-year-old widow who had been teaching for seventeen years.

In 1948, a few weeks before Christmas, Minnie was summoned from her first-grade class to the principal's office. His face a mask, the principal led her to the teacher's room, where two interrogators were waiting with a stenographer. Boom bang, the questions began. Was she a communist? Which meetings had she attended? Did she know any other teachers who were communists? The men referred to "a legal matter that would be taken up in court."

With these words, Minnie knew that her job was lost. It was just a few weeks after Alger Hiss's indictment for perjury, a year since the blacklist of the "Hollywood Ten" had begun. The mood in the country was ugly when it came to communist affiliations. The Soviet Union had become an adversary, its supporters, past and present, suspect. Even a teacher might mix in propaganda with the ABCs.

Shaken, Minnie left the school. She proceeded to the union office, where she composed a letter to Dr. William Jansen, Superintendent of Schools. "Dear Sir," the letter began, "a shocking thing happened to me in school today." Minnie went on to describe her experiences. "I have a highly satisfactory record as a teacher," she concluded. "No fault has ever been found with my conduct, professional and personal. . .I think it is highly unfair and improper to call a teacher out of a class and subject her to this type of questioning without any warning, or prior notice, or opportunity to consult with anyone for advice as to her legal rights."

As hundreds after Minnie were to discover, there were no "legal rights." Attorneys were not permitted. Later, when the investigation developed its own protocols, teachers were allowed to have a "teacher-adviser," a union member who was likely to know the ropes from having helped others.

Despite the brave front of the letter, written in the protest style so typical of the union, Minnie Gutride felt overwhelmed.

She returned to her Manhattan apartment, endured what was undoubtedly a sleepless night, and sometime the next morning, turned on the gas. Hours later, when a neighbor's knocks got no response, the superintendent opened the door. "The deceased was lying face down with her face on the gas jets, which were open," wrote the medical examiner.

Linda's file on Minnie Gutride contains a copy of her suicide note. *I have cancer and am too tired. Notify B. Arnest, 11 West 42nd St., NY, RE 6-8861. I leave everything to my mother, except where otherwise provided.* The medical examiner noted that the deceased had of late been suffering from depression.

Minnie Gutride's story could have been my mother's. Like Minnie, my mother was a widow, forty years old. Like Minnie, my mother had been teaching for seventeen years. And, Minnie, like my mother, had a little girl—but Minnie's child had been killed in an auto accident a few years earlier. The investigators may have noted this fact, or perhaps they weren't aware of it. Minnie wasn't important; she was just a place to begin.

Her insignificance fills me with rage. Like my mother, Minnie seems so defenseless, raked over, raped.

I can picture my mother meeting Minnie's fate, feeling dread in the pit of her stomach. You didn't need to be a "red" to be investigated. All you needed was a "leftist leaning." You only had to attend a meeting, distribute a leaflet, sign a petition, make remarks in the teacher's lunchroom that got reported to Mr. Saul Moskoff, the chief investigator, an assistant corporation counsel on loan to the Board of Education. Moskoff was a silky bulldog—smooth yet merciless in his persecutions, no transgression too small to be overlooked. One case he reported to the Board concerned a teacher whose ten-year-old daughter was found reading a "communist propaganda book" in school. The teacher was permitted to retire from the school system.

By 1952, Moskoff, who would later be rewarded with a judgeship, had accumulated index cards on 1,200 teachers. If my mother had lived, would there have been a card with her name?

I think back for signs of "redness" in her life.

I've read there were two ways of identifying a communist. One was the ever-present pile of petitions. We had that all right. The other was a subscription to the *Daily Worker*.

I don't remember ever seeing the *Worker* in our home.

My mother's paper, her bible really, was *PM,* a left-wing investigative newspaper. Like the *Worker*, *PM* was constantly up in arms, but its concerns were widespread, not just whatever happened to interest Moscow at the moment.

Looking at issues for just a few months in 1946, I learn that major Nazis are going unpunished, mass suicides are feared in DP camps, *Stars & Stripes*, the soldiers' newspaper, is being censored by the army, miners are striking over working conditions, meat packers the same, but housewives shouldn't bemoan the loss of meat. Instead, while cooking vegetables, they should ask why the meat industry hires so many exploited minority workers.

In *PM*, there was always something you should ask yourself, something you should be concerned about. The *Daily Worker*, as dull as it was doctrinaire, was a slacker in comparison.

But would my mother's reading materials have made a difference? If she wasn't a red herself, undoubtedly some of her union friends were. She might have attended a party function, common enough in the 1940s. And if, in the 1950s, someone remembered seeing her there, she would have rated a card from Saul Moskoff.

In the 1940s, few union members could have imagined the insanity of the 1950s. Everyone knew, of course, that the legislature's investigations would re-emerge in some form after the war. But nobody, liberal or red, could have predicted the relentlessness of the witch hunts. As one teacher put it in the 1950s, "I never dreamed that this thing would come up and hit me in the face."

Saul Moskoff and his crew were simply *beyond* imagining, except for one practiced worrier, one nightmare dreamer, my dear father. Looking back, I can see that, for him, Moskoff must have already been looming in the 1940s, a historical archetype: the grand inquisitor, destroyer of neat Bronx worlds.

Saul Moskoff fits in perfectly with my father's stockpile of anxieties; he is the model for every paranoid delusion, yet one day—and this is the amazing thing—Moskoff *will* be real, the nation paranoid.

I imagine a time when Moskoff's reality is only germinating. It's a spring night in 1945, a few weeks before my father kills himself. He comes home from a night shift at the post office, turns on a living room lamp, and sits on the tufted art deco sofa. In the dim light, he spies the petitions, the piles of *PM*, his collection of history books.

My father thinks about petitions, newspapers, and history. He recalls the radical "Wobblies," the International Workers of the World, and how the leadership was thrown into jail during World War I. He recalls the "red scare" after World War I, when the American Communist Party, newly delivered from a Moscow womb, was persecuted by government, press, and public.

After the war, there comes the reckoning.

My father knows it won't take long for the uneasy alliance between the Soviet Union and the United States to disintegrate. Fascism defeated, the Russians will be poised for expansion, free to pursue an aggressive course. Friends in the United States—party members, fellow travelers, even readers of *PM*—will all get painted red. Ruined.

This outcome my father sees as clearly as the waning moon outside the window. But he's not like other people. He can't tell himself that he's probably exaggerating. He can't think about something else, like how the Yankees are doing. He can only obsess.

The vision of a Moskoff-to-come contributes to my father's delusion that the FBI is on his trail because he lied about his age when applying for a post office job in his teens. He reasons that he's a liar married to a red. The FBI will get them both.

At dawn, when my mother starts to stir, he assaults her again with his many mantras. He begs her to leave the union. "Get out," he says, "get out." At least these are words I think I hear as I lie cowering in my bed. Right there, in 1945, my father can feel the crushing power of a Saul Moskoff. She'll lose her job; he'll lose his, because the United States Post Office will not care to employ the husband of a subversive. They will be drowned in a red, red sea.

My mother refuses to leave the union. It is, after all, her substitute love object, a place where she can be fulfilled.

I know she maintained her membership because, after her death, a union delegation visited and gave me a set of *Compton's Encyclopedia* with red leather bindings. I loved the smooth feel of the books, the scarlet color so cheery while working on a homework assignment—a color so appropriate if, indeed, the union was red.

My father was probably correct if he thought my mother might have wound up in Moskoff's files. Here's how I imagine a case against her could have developed:

One evening in 1944, my mother could have gotten invited to a Communist Party meeting at an apartment just a few blocks away, a "cell" consisting of ten teachers. They met one Tuesday a month, Tuesday, for some reason, being the hallowed night for Party meetings.

These comrades, all union teachers, were actually diverse in their thinking. Some joined because they were committed communists, others because the party's goals matched the union's at a particular moment. The dedicated communists thought they were using the union.

The dedicated unionists thought they were using the communists. All had been issued Party cards, which Saul Moskoff would later be able to trace.

The meeting took place in a sparsely decorated living room, on the walls two copies of Diego Rivera prints purchased at a Teachers Union bazaar. There were no refreshments because the hostess thought it "bourgeois" to ply guests with food. She had seen her mother slave her life away in a kitchen. For herself, she planned nobler things; she planned on getting the world.

The membership director, the woman who invited my mother to this imaginary meeting, collected monthly dues of twenty-five cents and stamped the membership booklets. My mother, a guest, paid no dues.

But it was no free ride. She was forced to listen to mind-blowing, arcane discussions, the twists and turns of Stalinist maneuvering, the "selling" to the credulous of party policy deadlier than anything members endured at the local Democratic Club, where you could at least get hot dogs and beer. To be a communist, you had to be short on appetite and long on patience, you had to be inured to boredom.

After the discussion, the literature director sold copies of the *Daily Worker* and arranged for the group to distribute fliers against racially biased hiring at a chain store the following weekend.

The literature director who prevailed upon my mother to take a flier was actually an undercover detective assigned to the Subversive Activities Unit of the New York Police Department. At home, she wrote down the names of everyone present. Years later, the detective's notes reached Saul Moskoff. That's how a name like my mother's could have wound up on one of his cards.

The card would have been useless if my mother died in 1946, six weeks after leaving me in the kitchen of our apartment wearing her mouton coast. Moskoff would have had to write "deceased," disappointing, really, because he couldn't get enough "subversives," enough Minnie Gutrides.

I'm glad my mother escaped Moskoff's clutches, but I can't help wondering how she would have behaved. The investigations were a test, and it's her character that interests me. I think about what I know so far: a caring heart (Emily's description), a humanist and loyal friend (Anna), a depressive (the medical record), a concealer (hider of a diabetic condition, mistress of mysterious funds), an ambivalent mother (my own memories).

But overriding these contradictions, the gestalt of the Teachers Union—justice, fairness, mutual support, blended with a strong dose of naiveté wholly ignorant of how power actually works. When the powerful pulled out their pincers, when everything was on the line, would she have turned on her friends?

I have to imagine her as being alive in the 1950s.

I have to conjure up a vision of those days.

In teacher lunchrooms throughout the city, union members and non-union teachers sit at different tables. Chickens are coming home to roost, the non-members cluck; not their chickens, thank goodness.

Union teachers talk of people being summoned and dismissed. The informers are those who keep their jobs—usually, but not always. Who can be trusted?

They live in fear of discovery. Everyone has some hidden, long-ago sin; even having lied on a driver's license application could be grounds for dismissal in this atmosphere. Or saying you were married to make things easier when really you were living "in sin." Or maybe you had an illicit abortion or a strange infection and were admitted to a sanitarium. Things like that could get you fired if you had ever lied about them, because perjurers, like communists, can't be allowed to teach.

My mother remembers my father's warnings. Now other husbands, live men, sane men, are using the same words: "Get out." Many people leave the union; membership plummets.

My mother stays because the union is now her first and greatest love. The psychiatrist ended their relationship, but her affair with the union can be trusted to go on and on.

Saul Moskoff doesn't get to my mother until 1954. He questions the leadership first. Then he gets down to the "names" named by others, people who were only spotted at a meeting or a rally. These cases are harder to prove, so each teacher has to be made to offer more names as a sign of loyalty. Names tighten the net around the next victim.

My mother finally receives the standard letter from the Superintendent of Schools as recorded in Linda's files: *You are hereby directed to report to my office, Room 1016, on April 24, 1954, at 3:15 p.m. It is my intention to ask you certain questions concerning your conduct, character, and fitness as a teacher, with particular reference to your alleged association with the Communist Party. You may bring with you a teacher/adviser of your own choice. Both you and your adviser may be excused from school early enough to reach my office at the stated time. If there is any difficulty about the excuse, please telephone my office, and it will be arranged.*

The principal excuses my mother early, of course. There's a troubled look in her eyes, the same look that principals are sporting all over the city. They're losing their best teachers. They're losing their pride, too, because most are too frightened to speak out.

On April 24, the chosen date of my imagining, my mother takes the subway to 10 Livingston Street in Brooklyn, offices of the Board of Education. She carries a pile of job performance reviews attesting to her skills as a teacher, and letters from parents, accumulated over the years, thanking her. She even brings along lesson plans, which show the originality of her thinking and a list of things she's done to create strong relationships with students.

"Pupil-teacher relationship" is a catch phrase of the union, a doctrine of belief. In the third grade, I had a mean teacher, and my mother once wrote her, in a chiding letter, *I don't understand the pupil-teacher relationship in your class. The children are afraid of you.* Shocking. There was nothing more important than making children feel secure, and that included getting raises for teachers. The union was more about children than anything else.

It's all so pathetic, the papers my mother is schlepping to No. 10, because no one cares. She might just as well drop the stuff on the subway tracks; it's not admissible evidence, and it might even be dangerous. Being a good teacher could be a sign of subversion.

Saul Moskoff greets my mother in an amiable fashion. No one expects the feared one to be such a charmer, but he is— gracious, fatherly, holding the chair for her, offering a glass of water.

Then he gets down to business.

In the paragraphs that follow, every word attributed to Moskoff was actually uttered by him in one interrogation or another, with the exception of the name and address of the cell I call the Bronx New World Club. My mother's words, of course, I'm making up, since she was not actually at the Board of Education but six feet below the ground, her body just about decomposed by then.

Moskoff begins with his standard disclaimer:

Moskoff: Mrs. Sonkin, this matter is confidential; it won't be known to anyone other than those officially connected with the board. I've been helping Dr. Jansen with this for some time. The Board of Ed adopted a policy in 1951 that said that present membership in the Communist Party is a basis for disqualification for continued employment. Past membership in and of itself does not require disqualification, but each case will be determined in the light of particular facts and circumstances, including the nature of the membership, its extent, its duration, and most important of all, whether or not there was a final, complete, and honest severance. The Board has said that there is an obligation on the part of teachers to be frank and candid in a discussion of the issues, and the Board expects that teachers, when questioned, will respond truthfully. This I merely say by way of caution and

> not for any other reason, because I don't anticipate for a moment that you will say anything less than the truth, but merely by way of caution. I can tell you that it is expected that the answers that you will make will be truthful, but if it should be found that your answers are not truthful, then you might be required to face whatever the consequences of that might be.

Now I have to decide how my mother would have responded. Most teachers fell into one of three categories—obsequious/submissive ("I'll do everything I can to be of assistance"), straightforward/cautious ("I understand"), or up- yours/rebellious ("You have no right to question me like this").

I'd like to think of my mother as rebellious, but she most likely would have been cautious. After all, she's alone with a daughter to support, and it's not certain how things will turn out. Perhaps she can save her job.

Moskoff (again): "If it should be found that your answers are not truthful, then you might be required to face whatever the consequences of that might be."

Sonkin: I understand.

Moskoff: Did you ever attend a workers school or

camp, ever take a course in Leninism or Marxism, ever subscribed to the Daily Worker, marched in a May Day parade?

He goes on to name a number of "workers' camps" in the Catskills. He doesn't name the camp in the Berkshires, the camp where my mother left me for the first time and where I learned the Soviet war anthem, "Meadowlands." Apparently, this camp isn't on the really red list; maybe it was merely pink.

Sonkin: No.
Moskoff: Did you ever attend a meeting of the Bronx New World Club?
Sonkin: (Confers with teacher adviser). I honestly don't recall.
Moskoff: Let me refresh your memory. On February 10, 1944, at the home of Mrs. Mickey Mouse at 1240 Mount Eden Avenue.
Sonkin: (Confers with teacher adviser). I believe I was there.
Moskoff: Now, would you please let me know who were the members of the Bronx New World Club. I am being perfectly frank. This is more in the nature of testing your good faith rather than for the purpose of accumulating

information. In other words, I expect you to tell the truth.

This is the $64.00 question, to use the words of one teacher who cited the grand prize on a popular radio quiz show. In those days, $64.00 was a lot of money. In those days, naming names was worth more than cash.

But my mother's best friends were union members. These were women who helped when her mother was ill, supported her in a difficult marriage, traded advice about childcare, summered in the Berkshires. They were a substitute family, perhaps even more important than a job.

Sonkin: (Confers with teacher adviser). I can make a statement about myself. I cannot make a statement about others.

Moskoff: Now, look, Mrs. Sonkin, I am trying to help you. I hope you realize that. I get some satisfaction out of being able to say to a teacher, "Go home and forget about the whole thing," more than I do out of anything else, but you've got to help out, too.

Sonkin is silent. He mistakes her silence for hesitation.

> *Moskoff*: Now, would you be good enough to tell me who it was who were members of this Bronx New World Club, bearing in mind that no harm will befall Mrs. Mouse, or any of these people, if they are not and have not been for a time members of the Communist Party.

It would be so easy, no harm will come to them, her job will be guaranteed—just a name to show her good faith. After all, he says, he already *knows* the names. No one will think the worse of her. Everyone is doing it, everyone.

But she'll lose her friends. She'll fall deeper into the pit of regret that already imprisons her. She'll have to look at herself in the mirror, in that same bathroom where her husband stashed a gun and her father continues to stockpile disgusting medications. Only the bathroom will be smaller and colder. And she'll be seeing herself differently forevermore.

And then, I hear the word "No." Her dust is speaking—no, no, no—as loud as Molly Bloom's "yes." "No," seeping out of her grave, bouncing off the tombstone, ricocheting through the cemetery, making visitors shiver.

Saul Moskoff looks sad; such an unwise decision on the part of Mrs. Sonkin. He only wanted to help

She stares at him, reflecting that he's only the most recent in a series of men who have messed with her mind—her father, her husband, her psychiatrist, and now Torquemada himself. Like other union teachers, those who predeceased the investigations and those who suffered through them, she views him with disgust from the grave. My mother claims that dates don't matter—she was *there* in Moskoff's Star Chamber at No. 10 Livingston Street. They were *all* there. Don't forget us, Minnie Gutride says.

9
Clara And Theresa

AFTER SHE LEFT ME in the summer of 1946, my mother went to stay with her brother, Bernie, and his wife, Theresa. Five weeks later, Theresa had my mother admitted to the West Hill Sanitarium in Riverdale, where she died. I know Theresa made the arrangements because her name is on the bill in my mother's file in the Bronx Surrogate's Court. *Mrs. Theresa Paley, $99.38, past due*, notes West Hill.

Mrs. Theresa Paley knew how my mother had managed to expire of diabetes in a mental institution. She knew whether there was a rapist, a lover, or nothing at all except depression, guilty memories, and future fears. Theresa could fit the pieces together; maybe she even helped to put them in place.

Theresa was also younger than my mother and might

still be alive. Yet I hesitated to search because, to my mind, Theresa was a witch and, in the custody battle that followed my mother's death, she and Bernie, her partner in black magic, had tried to carry me away from the Sonkins.

They failed, but eight years later, something else happened. Bernie died, leaving Theresa to care for Louis, his increasingly confused father. Theresa convinced Louis to turn his personal assets over to her and to sign a will she'd written, making herself his heir.

Louis had two grandchildren—Janet, my age, the daughter of Theresa and Bernie; and me. At least half of his money should have been mine. Louis always said it would be when he visited me at the Sonkins. He'd put his hand in his pocket, pull out a bill or two, and then put them back. He wanted to give me something, but the pain of giving was too great. So he'd tell Philip and Kate that I was in his will and, then, looking relieved, pop a Chiclet in his mouth and head for the door.

The will was the only love Louis ever demonstrated, but his plans were thwarted by Theresa, who got all the money—at least, that's what Aunt Sylvia said. But when I pried into the records of the Bronx Surrogate's Court, I learned differently. I found that Theresa had never probated the dubious will because of a challenge from Uncle Robert. The court had allowed Robert's attorney to track down the assets she'd taken, and a fair share of the monies had been added to those my parents had left me.

I'm certain Sylvia had misunderstood what happened because of the extreme power she ascribed to Theresa. For me, too, Theresa was a threat.

It tormented me to think that my mother, in her final illness, had been forced to turn to a woman who would betray her child's interests. Surely they had nothing in common, the left-wing school teacher and the hard-nosed gold digger. My mother had lots of friends, women who worked with her in the union, went with her to summer camp, chatted with her on the phone. How sad to have to rely on someone who hadn't really cared. How desperate to seek solace in a witch's chamber.

For decades, I'd made it a rule never to think about Theresa or my mother, particularly the two of them together, because of the way it made my stomach churn.

When I decided to search for my mother, the churning came back, a fifty-year case of acid indigestion. Finding Theresa should have been my first move, but I made it the last. A witch's power increases with age. Theresa in her eighties was still to be feared.

At last, I get up the courage to send for Bernie's death certificate, which notes where he's buried. From the cemetery clerk, I learn there are two adjoining graves, one occupied by Bernie, the other unoccupied. The person responsible for upkeep is a Mrs. Theresa Levinson in California, and until seven years ago she'd been paying regularly.

It's no surprise that Theresa remarried. She was only in her early forties when Bernie died in 1954. But why did she stop paying? Perhaps she forgot about Bernie and his forlorn grave. More likely, she was dead herself, resting in the Levinson family plot, so far from the Bronx, her Bernie love, and all memories of her troubled sister-in-law.

The Social Security Administration maintains an index of recipients who have died. The *Death Index*, available on the Internet, lists several Theresa Levinsons, all dead within the past eight years, none having died in California.

I theorize that Theresa split from Mr. Levinson, or he died, and his family tossed her out, after fights over the will, of course, the Theresa specialty. They packed her suitcase and pushed her toward the door. She trotted away like Baba Yaga, the wrinkled old witch of Russian fairy tales, a hood obscuring her face.

Good God, what ill feeling I have toward this woman, just because my mother was forced to rely on her, just because she caused my stalwart Sonkin family so much pain!

I send for the death certificates of the departed

Theresa Levinsons. One of them, a woman who died in Florida, has an Italian maiden name, close enough to Corleone to send a shiver through me. My Theresa, no doubt.

I try to imagine Theresa's Corleone roots.

I envision the family on a spring day in the 1920s. They're in the dining room, seated on red damask chairs around a huge oak table. In the matching sideboard, silver-plate pitchers and mounds of artificial fruit. An imitation Tiffany chandelier flickers overhead. On the wall, a votive candle, and a saint's picture, Nicholas, patron saint of thieves as well as poor children.

The Corleones have been assigned a rub-out. Theresa's brother, Guido, the man listed on her death certificate as providing information, is to meet the target at a restaurant, chat for awhile, then go to the bathroom and retrieve a gun planted behind the toilet. "You must move quickly, Guido, my son," says the father. "There's an old Sicilian proverb, 'He who delays arrives early for his own funeral.' Do you understand?"

Guido nods nervously; he's messed up several previous jobs.

On this one, all goes well until the bathroom, where he decides to take a leak before getting the gun. Afterwards, he combs his hair and readjusts the clasp of the gold chain he wears around his neck. He bends to flush the toilet and something terrible happens. Instead of tightening the clasp, he's loosened it; the monster adornment falls into the bowel, causing the toilet to overflow. The restaurant owner pushes open the door and finds Guido up to his knees in water, a dripping gun in his hand. The proprietor is furious. There have been five rub-outs in the past eight months. He's even thought about putting a sign over the toilet—*Don't even think about it.* Unceremoniously, he ejects Guido as the target and his companions watch with mocking eyes. "What a *goumba,*" they comment.

The Corleones are disgraced. Everyone knows they're mere Mafia wannabes, hopeless, harmless.

Making Guido a nincompoop diffuses the threat I feel from the family, gives me the courage to write to him: *You don't know me, but your sister, Theresa Levinson, was once married to my uncle, Bernie T. Paley, the brother of my mother, Clara Paley Sonkin. I am interested in getting in touch with my cousin, Janet Paley, the daughter of Theresa and Bernie. If you can give me Janet's address, or pass this letter along, I would be most appreciative.*

Janet, I reason, may remember something of my mother's final days, even though she was, like me, only a child at the time. I mail the letter on a Monday. Wednesday evening the phone rings, and a throaty, intimate voice says, "Jean, two weeks ago I dreamed that you were looking for me. I said to my husband, 'My cousin wants to talk to me.'"

Janet doesn't find it strange that I have contacted her after all these years. As with Emily and Anna, I get the impression she's been waiting and, in her case, consulting the stars for the hour of our reconnect.

Her low voice bubbles with friendliness. She ticks off her family—three children, a grandchild, a doctor husband, and the successful retail store she ran in New Jersey. She lives currently in Florida, a few hours from Uncle Guido.

Janet doesn't ask, but after a while I feel compelled to mention my ostensible reason for calling, the breast cancer gene and Minnie's death. "Oh no, my dear," says Janet, "our grandma didn't die of breast cancer. She had a gall bladder operation, things got botched up, and she died of peritonitis. Whenever my mother heard about someone with gall bladder trouble, she'd say, 'Get the best doctor. I'll never forget what happened to my dear mother-in-law.'"

Okay, so they told a child a cancer-concealing fable, par for the course in those days, no reason to assume a family pattern of subterfuge. But I'm prepared to hear strange tales, evidence of pain. And I do.

When Minnie was sick with the gall bladder botch-up, Louis refused to hire a nurse, Janet reports. He said there was no point, she'd die anyway, so my mother did the nursing. I'd learned from Emily that my mother had taken a leave to nurse Minnie, but not the reason why—Louis's bottomless selfishness, the pivotal influence in the Paley family drama. As a toddler, it affected even me, because my mother was often absent, tending to Minnie.

Louis, Louis, you made everything grim, killed love before it even got started.

Janet, too, bears Louis' scars. "He lived with us after your mother died, and it was tough. He'd sit in front of the television set, shouting, 'Shit, shit, shit,' and my father would yell at him to shut up. They hated one another. Louis always said he'd spit on my father's grave, and you know what? He did." Her voice grows softer, more confiding, "Literally, he did."

I see it happening. A frigid December day, a suburban cemetery, shortly after Bernie's funeral. At the gate, Louis hops out of a cab, still disputing the fare. The cabbie drives off in a blaze of expletives. Louis, bent with age, white hair flowing, trudges up the path to Bernie's grave. He plans to leave, not a stone, by Jewish custom the sign that someone has visited, but another remembrance. He unbuttons his overcoat, fumbles with his fly, and finally unzips it, revealing an ancient penis, corroded, like a dead-white worm. The cold makes peeing painful, but he endures, producing a steady, even stream. "This is for you, Bernie," he prays. "Who fought me, stole from me, killed my Clara, after you took her away to make her well. What happened to my Clara? Piss on you, Bernie, you *pischaka*."

What happened to my Clara? The prayer is mine. For an answer, I need to get closer to Janet than a phone conversation and the exchange of photographs that follows. I need to talk face to face with the witch's child.

A few months later, I fly to Florida, ostensibly to see friends, but also to "squeeze in" a visit to Janet. I'll try to drop by, if I can, I tell her on the phone. If I can. I schedule everything, flight, motel, car rental, even weather reports, so there's no way I can miss.

As with my visit to Anna, I leave Solomon behind. I need to be in the 1940s, the grimy archaeological past he cannot share. "Be careful," he says as he hugs me goodbye. "Be sure to call." Of course I'll call, but he means, *Call right away if you're falling apart*, because that's what he's afraid will happen. Most people view me as solid, but Solomon recognizes my fragility; he's had to live with the consequences of choosing a mate who survived a childhood "mess." He knows I can crack wide open at any moment. On the plane, I feel his hand gripping my shoulder, ready to save me from any loss of altitude.

Before seeing Janet, I visit a Sonkin cousin, and the conversation turns to my current mission. Helen remembers the custody battle. "Your Grandma Kate was fierce. She said she'd never let the Paleys have you, that she'd flee the country first." A thrill of recognition shoots through me, the possessive love I always felt from the Sonkins. Of course, Kate would have done anything, did do whatever was asked of her. Starting kindergarten, I suffered fierce separation anxiety. Each morning I'd halt at the iron school doors, the doors of a prison, I was certain, and shriek. If I stepped inside, I'd be swallowed up, destroyed. My mother had to be at her job, so Kate sat in Miss Lauricella's classroom for months, until I felt secure enough for her to leave. How much cleaning, shopping, and baking of *rugelach* went untended while she sat there? No matter, I was Number One with the Sonkins, a feeling I never got from the Paleys, including my mother.

The night before my visit to Janet, I toss and turn, reviewing the phone conversations that followed the first one.

I'd learned something of my cousin's life growing up in the Paley household. As a father, Bernie was remote and dictatorial, not unlike Louis, the model he had ostensibly rebelled against. Bernie's major interaction with his daughter was to teach Louis's values. Each morning, he'd ask Janet if he could borrow a dollar from the brown jar that contained her allowance. Each evening, he'd return the dollar with five cents interest and an inquiring look on his face. Did she understand the lesson? Money rules.

"I only got to know him in the three years before his death," Janet told me. Then Bernie was ill, bedridden, willing to open up emotionally to his daughter. Before that, Janet felt closed out by the intensity of her parents' relationship.

Bernie and Theresa were perpetual lovers and, though "they fought all the time," they were totally involved with one another. Theresa admitted she would have preferred avoiding motherhood. She said that Carmella, her daughter by her first marriage when she was sixteen, was the result of "my being too dumb at the time to know what to do." Janet had been "a case of the flu."

It didn't sound like a jolly household, and Janet practically lived next door at the apartment of the boy she later married. I wasn't surprised to learn that Janet had been estranged from Theresa in her mother's later years. "She got too crazy," Janet said.

But despite their difficulties, Janet loved her mother, took pride in Theresa's adventures, her four husbands, her fierce lust for life. "I buried my mother under all her names, because that *was* her—Theresa Corleone, Davis, Paley, Konigsberg, Levinson. A glamour queen. Let's face it, she was the Joan Crawford of the Bronx."

As I drive to Janet's house, I ponder the Crawford image, so disturbing, so on the mark.

I remember seeing a Joan Crawford movie in the year after my father died, something about a woman who has to hide her past and undergoes a face-changing operation. Lights glare down, instruments shimmer, the surgeon addresses the nurse in majestic tones, the voice of powerful men in 1940s movies. With this voice they advise, direct, and ultimately save women from themselves, from troublesome faces. Later on in the movie, when the bandages come off, the face unveiled is that of JC—to me, insincere, monstrous. Even as a child, I sensed there was something wrong with the actress who had that face, old or new.

The film, with its ambiguities of identity, frightened me. My mother tried to soothe with an explanation of special effects. There really wasn't an operation, she said in her rational way. They simply stopped the camera every few minutes to change the make-up. Everything I saw on screen was not real. Not real? Then why was Crawford crying so much, why were her lips so smeared with lipstick, her eyebrows so dark and menacing? And what about those *bandages?* In the middle of the night, I gazed down at my mother's pillow. I wanted to make sure her face hadn't changed.

As I drive to Janet's house, I have the same eerie feeling of dislocation that film produced. I see myself moving into harm's way, beyond the bounds of Sonkin protection, and I realize that the person driving the car is nine-year-old Sara Jean.

Happily, Sara Jean finds nothing ominous about Janet's house. It's a pretty Florida ranch on a pretty Florida street, a neat subdivision out of a Spielberg movie. There's even an adorable boy, pug-nosed, red-helmeted kid riding about on his bicycle, waiting, perhaps, for ET.

Inside the house, Florida colors of pink and green, a leather sectional sofa facing a television set, sunlight streaming through glass doors that lead to the rear patio. The landscaping isn't as easy to maintain as one might think, says Janet's husband. Amid the lushness, there are pests, armadillos, who chomp up the grass, creating holes that can cause twisted ankles and worse. So there's danger here after all, or perhaps merely annoyances. It depends on how much gets covered over, how much truth remains.

Janet is a tall, slender woman. "I was always a string bean," she says, bustling about with a capable air. With ease, she disposes of frequent phone queries from the staff of the mail order business she manages. "Well, go ahead, order more," she says, running her fingers through her long blonde hair and shrugging her shoulders at me.

She insists that she looks like her father, but I see hints of Theresa in her vivacious brown eyes.

She directs me to the dining table, while she carts from the kitchen a ton of cold cuts—corned beef, pastrami, roast beef, turkey, and her own homemade chopped liver. "You can't buy the good stuff around here," she says, spreading the sensuous mixture on crackers, putting the crackers on my plate, watching me finish them off.

Janet is a nonstop talker, an endearing combination of practicality—the successful businesswoman who learned Bernie's lessons well—and the romantic who dreams of long-lost cousins and embellishes with color the family's rather squalid history of secrets and squabbles.

Examples:

Janet didn't know that Bernie had been married previously until she helped her mother clean out legal papers shortly before her death. "Why didn't you tell me?" Janet asked. "It only lasted nine months," Theresa said. "It didn't really happen."

Janet's half-sister, Carmella, didn't know she wasn't Bernie's child until she applied for a marriage license and had to produce a birth certificate. Bernie always planned to adopt Carmella but didn't want to spend the money to file the papers.

Bernie, in Louis' later years, finally managed to "retire" his father from the business. How this was done, Janet doesn't say. She doesn't have to.

Minnie's sister, Aunt Mollie Minkin, the hysterical lady with the mole, cut her husband, Izzy, out of her will. Fortunately, Izzy died first, so he didn't have to suffer the consequences of being disinherited. The consequences of living with Mollie, Janet doesn't describe.

Theresa entrusted her relatives to purchase mausoleum space for her "overlooking the ocean." But Theresa's resting place has no ocean view. "I wouldn't be surprised if they pocketed part of the money," Janet says.

I realize that Janet is recounting these stories to put me at ease, make me part of the group.

"You know how families are," she says pleasantly.

I don't know; the Sonkins, not perfect by any means, would not have cheated one another. They saved me from that kind of family knowing. But my mother knew—plenty. She was one of the Paleys, and when I think of her with them, when I think of her palling around with Theresa, I don't like her at all.

My mother, her mother—that's the discussion Janet and I have been waiting to have.

I tell her that I never knew what happened to my mother after she went to Bernie and Theresa in the summer of 1946. She simply vanished from my life, and I wanted to fill in the gaps now.

"I can see that you've been hurting," Janet says, shepherding a slice of corned beef around her plate.

She recalls that my mother was physically ill with diabetes "from the stress of your father's death. She stayed in my room, and I moved in with Carmella." I picture my mother lying in bed in a small room at the end of long hall, the room where Janet and I used to play with her ample supply of toys. It would be so inviting there, to curl up in a child's room and become a child again, will yourself into nothingness, after losing a husband, being raped, having a pregnancy terminated, being unable to put one foot in front of the other.

Weeks, though—there were *weeks* of being sick. Unlikely that it would take that long to get *diabetes* under control. Could there have been something else, I ask, an unusual experience or an infection?

Janet looks perplexed. "Well, diabetes is a sort of infection," she says.

And was it diabetes, then, that sent my mother to the mental institution where she died?

Janet looks shocked. "No, no, my dear, it was diabetes, but she didn't go to a *mental* institution. It was a rehabilitation place, like for physical therapy, where you go to get your health back."

What made me think that Bernie and Theresa would

tell the truth to a child? Any of the things I think might have happened would be far worse than Minnie's breast cancer, and they'd covered that up. They must have tiptoed around, whispering, waiting until Janet went off to school to discuss what was really wrong with Clara. Janet is no repository of information; she knows less than I do—or does she?

Her face is perfectly placid, honest. What she remembers, apparently, is not how my mother died, but the vivid aftermath, the raw emotion she witnessed from her parents.

"My father lay on the floor and howled,"Janet says. "Just howled. I remember that, the way he cried. He loved her so much."

Loved her? The possibility has never entered my mind, because it turns Bernie into a human being. And if he loved her, he might have loved me too, wanted me.

Janet seems to sense what I'm thinking."You may not know this, but your mother. . ." She pauses warily, but I'm staring so hard she's forced to continue. "Well, your mother left instructions, a piece of paper saying that you should be with us. My father had the document. The judge decided against us, though, because my parents had an intermarriage. And there wasn't any religion practiced in our house."

I ponder the possible veracity of this. The files in the

Bronx Surrogate's Court contain no such document. Perhaps the paper was of dubious legality—like the will Theresa would later cook up for Louis—so Bernie never introduced it to the court. Perhaps the paper never existed except as a way of explaining the custody battle to Janet. Perhaps Janet dreamed up the paper to demonstrate her parents' good intentions toward me.

But something about her version of the judge's reasoning resonates. In the late 1940s, intermarrying made a person damaged goods, like getting raped or going to a mental institution, or having diabetes. Add to this previous marriages for both partners—more damage—and one of them was a contortionist, but the judge wouldn't have known about that.

Otherwise, objectively, Bernie and Theresa, a young couple with children, one the same age as the minor in question, would appear the superior choice. Philip and Kate were elderly, their adult children, Robert and Sylvia, unmarried, future plans uncertain, not the best bet. Except that the minor is tied to them at the hip.

Seeing the Sonkins at a disadvantage, I feel a stab of fear, as if that document could be produced at any moment, as if Janet could retrieve it from her neat linen closet and force me to stay forever in her pink-and-green house, never more to see Solomon, my children, or grandchildren.

The fear is wrenching, a replay of the custody hearing, which was, in its uncertainty, just as agonizing as my parents' deaths. Memories of that time are black or blurry and often blurry black, a smudged negative that cannot be developed.

Among the blurs, me talking to the judge in his chambers, a room with leather bound books but not as many books as Uncle Robert has everywhere in his room, on the desk, shelves, floor—books stuffed with notes and newspaper clippings. I find the musty odor of Robert's books comforting, the way it lingers in his tweed jacket, even overpowering his after-shave, *eau de Robert*. I can see the judge's mouth moving, feel my mouth getting drier. I say I want Robert, not the other uncle.

If I'd thought my mother wanted Bernie to have me, I'd have hated her. If she intended to keep me from the Sonkins, why had she used their baby-sitting services so liberally, bound me to them? Why hadn't she asked Theresa to sit in Miss Lauricella's classroom?

Janet can't imagine the childish thoughts flooding through my head, and she certainly doesn't know the hostility I feel toward her parents. Aware of their shortcomings, she's nonetheless intensely loyal. Bernie and Theresa wanted me desperately, she says.

"I never heard from your father after the custody case," I counter, and maybe I sound a bit hurt.

Janet stares. Her voice becomes more sympathetic, sisterly. "My dear, it's because you don't remember." She tells me there was a meeting "in a neutral place." Kate and Philip were there, Bernie and Theresa, and Janet herself. Bernie told me why he had fought for custody; he said how much he had wanted to have me.

I don't press Janet for details, although there's the tiniest flicker of recognition. I can't remember a place, but I can remember a feeling—the feeling of wanting to push Bernie away for creating the custody fight. All these years, I resented his lack of contact but, in truth, *I* didn't want to see *him*. I might even have told him to keep away, kissed him off, the way I did in my fantasy at the Bronx Surrogate's Court. Currently, I want to find my mother but without running into Bernie and Theresa. Yet the three could well be inseparable. To know one, I'm going to have to accept the other two.

Janet's looking straight at me. "You know, my father and your mother were very close," she says. "And my mother loved your mother, even more than she loved her sisters. She gave me the middle name of Clara after your mother."

I'm stunned. The custom of Ashkenazi Jews is to name children for dead people. To name for a living person is to shorten that person's life, unthinkable. But, of course, Theresa was a Corleone, not an Ashkenazi Jew.

"My mother said she didn't care what anyone thought," Janet says. "She wanted to honor your mother and that was that."

Didn't care what anyone thought—well, that sounds like Theresa. But the rest of it, the loving part, could that be true? If it is, and Theresa was a genuine friend to my mother—a possibility I'd never considered—I'm going to have to promote her out of the witch brigade.

Janet suggests that we look through her photograph album. She values family and, by reconnecting, I've expanded hers considerably. Before I made contact, she knew nothing about Anna and Emily or their father, Minnie's brother, Abe, and she knew little about Minnie's parents, Sholem and Sarah.

I'd sent her the photo taken at Sholem and Sarah's fiftieth-anniversary party—the one Emily unearthed for me—and now I'm touched to see that it's first in the album.

Next come photos of Theresa's parents—the mother a saint, the father mean as nails, Janet says, rather like the Paley family, I think. The Corleones had fifteen children. You'd have to be pretty strong to survive in a family like that.

Once again, I imagine that Corleone conference, only now it's crowded at the oak dining table. Siblings compete for attention, favors, money—how they love money.

They smile at their mother, soothe their father's anger, and learn his lessons—go after what you want, be ruthless if you have to; even when it's family, take care of yourself first. I'm beginning to have a better understanding of Theresa.

As Janet turns the pages, the pug-nosed boy I'd seen outside comes into the house. He's her grandson, and he's fascinated by the 1940s photographs—women with short skirts and pompadour hair-dos, Catskills bungalows, Bronx apartment houses, his grandmother and me bundled up in woolen snowsuits, Janet's curly locks peeking out from a hood, a stringbean Shirley Temple.

We tell Raymond how children helped to win the war in the 1940s. We separated the silver foil in cigarette packs from its paper backing, saved the foil, and when we got enough, rolled it into balls. We saved newspapers, too, and the fat left over from cooking. The fat we gave to the butcher for extra red tokens, "points" they were called, so that you could buy more meat. The newspapers and the silver balls got turned in at a center of some sort. We carted it there in the little red wagons kids used to have; even if you lived in an apartment, you had a wagon.

Raymond looks incredulous, as if we come from another planet, and we explain wartime deprivations. You couldn't get all the meat you wanted then; things were rationed. He wants to know what "rationed means," and what did the army do with the silver and the fat. The silver was for parachutes, Janet thinks, or to line radar screens, I think, and as for the fat, we don't have the slightest idea.

We're laughing—those times seem absurd, yet their poignant bravery resonates. Even little children were expected to understand the need for sacrifice. In school we learned a song about rationing: "I like sugar and things that are sweet /And here in this country there's plenty to eat /But Uncle Sam says, 'Take care, take care, / Don't waste any food that we all must share.'"

I'm looking hard at the photographs, hoping they'll shed some light on my mother. I remember how she gave me the sense of working for a new world, a better one, where children wouldn't have to save silver foil, and even more important, where other children, far away, wouldn't be starved, bombed, or murdered in concentration camps. We knew about the camps because my mother's favorite crusading newspaper, *PM*, published the truth about what was happening to the Jews way before anyone else.

I recall my mother's ideas better than the woman herself, so any scrap from Janet, any chance word she drops, helps to fill up my canvas, a snail-paced Jackson Pollock, drip by drip.

Raymond spies Grandma Theresa posing on a diving

board in a 1940s bathing suit he finds amusing.

"The bathing suit was your mother's," Janet says to me. "It was an athlete's suite, brown wool. My mother wore it forever, and then Carmella."

I remember that my mother was a good athlete, terrific at swimming and tennis. In the summer after my father's death, she learned to golf. We'd take the elevated train to a public golf course in Mosholu Park, my mother in a playsuit and golf shoes, a bag of clubs slung over her shoulder. If the train wasn't crowded, we'd prop the bag against an empty seat, and I'd sit so that I could keep the bag from falling over.

I'd think about how my father and I used to take that train and stand peering out the window of the first car, pretending to be driving, balancing ourselves, so that we survived each wild turn with assurance. I would never do that again; I was too old, and he was too dead. I was stuck with golf. At the clubhouse, I sat around and waited for my mother, bored, but wanting her to have a good time.

For the first time, I wonder what she did on that golf course. Take lessons, practice her stroke? And if she played a game, as she must have sooner or later, who was her partner? Blurry black—someone there, someone we'd meet up with, or maybe not, maybe just us.

The bathing suit seems more concrete than the memory that eludes me. I want to get my hands on that suit, rub my fingers over the wool, feel my mother in the skeins, all her proud athleticism for me alone. Theresa, the thief, stole the suit that should have been mine, took my mother away.

But Theresa, too, may have needed a memory, a trophy of her attempts to save my mother. Or maybe it was a hair shirt, a monument to failure. Not likely. Theresa wasn't the hair shirt type; you can't be when you're in a contest with all those siblings—pause for a second of guilt, and you're done in.

"What's this?" Raymond asks. He's spied a photo hidden behind the others; all we can see is the top of a woman's head. Janet retrieves that photo and two others; all include my mother. She is the woman whose head Raymond spotted. The pictures were taken in August 1945, three months after my father hurled himself from the roof, three months after she cradled his body in the courtyard.

In the photos, Theresa and Clara are visiting Bernie, a member of the National Guard, at an army camp.

In one picture, my mother and Theresa are in front of Bernie's tent, pointing to the company banner, *Eighth New York.* In another, my mother stands between Bernie—slightly paunchy, hair thinning, but otherwise the perfect GI—and a thin Sinatra-like soldier who was

Bernie's best pal. Like Bernie, Frank Roberto has one arm around my mother, and I dislike him immediately, the way he slouches, looks disinterested, and probably is, because he's been roped into cheering her up. I hate his being so close, though he scarcely seems to be touching her. Roberto aside, I'm struck by the physical similarities between my mother and Bernie—same mouth, nose, cheekbones, high forehead, same furrows, even, in the brow, on the same threshold of middle age.

My mother looks fresh and shiny, spiffed up for the occasion, probably by Theresa. Her hair is tied back tight with a floppy velvet bow so that the heart shape of her face is emphasized. She's wearing a casual, loose-fitting pants suit—belted jacket with a V-neck collar, a Katharine Hepburn look except for the fact that my mother, unlike Hepburn, has hips. Theresa's outfit couldn't present more of a contrast—short pleated skirt, Mexican peasant blouse, necklace with large wooden beads, and above each ear, glistening amid her jet black hair, an artificial flower, the sort Dorothy Lamour might wear in the South Seas.

I notice that my mother's left hand still bears a wedding ring, and her face—oh, her face—has the wry smile and lost look she often wore during her last year of life, the year when the two of us were alone together.

If the two women, Clara and Theresa, aren't close friends, they're giving a pretty good imitation. They seem totally at ease with one another, and I reflect that this expedition could not have been their first. It's likely that they visited Bernie at camp before, even while my father was alive. Probably they go to the movies or on shopping trips, even though my mother isn't a major shopper. She makes her own clothing and mine—and even if she did shop, she wouldn't shop where Theresa does, where they sell those outfits that smug Jewish matrons used to call "guinea taste."

"Guinea taste": The words always made me shudder, they sounded so mean, and suddenly they explain the closeness between my mother and Theresa. Each was a stranger in her husband's family; each had committed a crime. Theresa's crime was being Italian; even the Bronx Surrogate's Court agreed that was a bad thing. My mother's crime was concealing her diabetes, and the Sonkins never forgot, because for them forgetting was an impossible thing.

Two guinea hens, off center. Their outsider status drew the two together. In Theresa, my mother found the perfect confidante.

With her, no need to be the teacher, the intellectual, the social activist. She could relax and just be Bernie's sister, with all the family baggage that entailed. No need to excuse her personal behavior, as with the high-minded Anna—"You didn't know I was like that, did you?" She could talk openly about my father, his illness, her grief, the things she did to fill up the loneliness, the men who helped or hurt her, because Theresa knew about men.

With Theresa, my mother could be sick, depressed, a burden, because she had carried Theresa's burdens. She made Theresa welcome, convinced Minnie to act as if she accepted her, aided Bernie in the ongoing manipulations of Louis. My mother had been a good scout, and Theresa owed her.

My mother wasn't forced to turn to Theresa. Theresa was her first choice. She needed to rely on the strength of a practiced survivor.

As my mother's condition worsened, Theresa took charge. She got her admitted to West Hill, a sanitarium "for nervous, mental, drug, and alcoholic patients," according to an ad in an old medical directory. West Hill was a discreet haven for celebrity alcoholics (the local folks say that Peter Lorre was once a patient). In 1963, when West Hill closed down and Manhattan College bought the property, a student reporter described a place "right out of Virgil's idylls." On fifty rolling acres, there were winding roads, gurgling springs, fountains, waterwheels, and a quaint old footbridge. Flowers, waterfowl, and other birds abounded.

In that "dreamily romantic" setting, the total opposite of Dr. Wallace's utilitarian commune, my mother spent her final days. She might have been in the main building, a Victorian mansion with a welcoming if somewhat Gothic aspect, or in one of the luxurious patient cottages. No matter where, West Hill was not set up to handle diabetes, post-abortion complications, an infection stemming from rape, or anything else I might imagine. The only non-psychiatrist on staff was a cardiologist who was required to monitor electro-shock treatments. This man would later sign my mother's death certificate, noting the cause of death as diabetes mellitus, a disease with which he must have had little experience.

One West Hill specialty, though, was discretion, and Theresa, in placing my mother there, was protecting herself, the first rule in the survivor's code.

Before visiting Janet, I had tried to get a look at the former West Hill property. Currently, it belongs to an exclusive day school, with *Private Property* signs and guards at the gates. Reasonable enough, since schools cannot allow strangers to wander about.

But I didn't see myself as a stranger. I had a vested interest in the place.

I called the office and said I was doing research on West Hill. A pleasant voice thought a tour might be arranged, but later, the head of security turned me down. "We're doing construction," he said, "and it's inconvenient to show people around right now. Perhaps you could call back in a few months." I got the feeling the answer would always be no. I must have sounded pretty weird, wanting to see West Hill thirty-five years after the place disappeared. Smarter to say I was considering the school for my grandson, who was moving East from Chicago, Los Angeles, or some other faraway place.

But it wasn't a grandmother who made that call. It was Sara Jean, cut off again from her mother, locked out of her death, as of her life.

On a winter Saturday, I drove to the property and parked a few blocks from the main gate. The guards, I figured, wouldn't be so alert on a non-school day. Slowly, I walked down the street, running my fingers along the fence, peering through the bars. I could see the winding roads described by the student newspaper, the rows of evergreens, the eccentric main building stationed like a sentinel near the entrance. It was a fiercely cold day, and as I peered closer, my cheek stuck to the iron fence. Stung, I pulled away, and tears sprang to my eyes for my brief discomfort, for my mother's extended pain.

Somewhere amid that carefully tended beauty, she had died, all alone. She turned her face to the wall and simply sobbed her life away. This was my vision, because I couldn't imagine Bernie and Theresa truly taking care of her. I thought they simply put her someplace, and that was that, because they were too callous to do much more.

Talking with Janet, I can see that she wasn't alone. Most likely, her friend Theresa was with her, badgering the cardiologist, watching the deterioration, all the while holding my mother's hand, reporting back to Bernie, who, according to Janet, was too fearful to visit a hospital, figuring out what story to tell Janet and Carmella, maybe even having a thought about Sara Jean.

Theresa did the best she could according to her survivor's view of things.

A biography tells the story of Georgiana, Duchess of Devonshire, an eighteenth-century beauty and leading society figure. In 1782, Lady Elizabeth (Bess) Foster, a divorcée with a checkered past, wormed her way into the heart and household of the duchess, forming a friendship that would last for twenty-four years. Bess bore two children in secret to Georgiana's husband, the Duke, but even when the Duchess learned of the indiscretions, the two women remained close. Everyone else in the family regarded Bess as an adventuress, yet Georgiana relied on her.

As a final act of friendship, Georgiana left her private papers to her, so that Bess would become indispensable and not be expelled from the Devonshire estate. Bess arranged Georgiana's papers to suit herself, destroying or keeping letters to leave a record detrimental to Georgiana's reputation and beneficial to her own.

In this, says biographer Amanda Foreman, "She was not being deliberately unfaithful to Georgiana; she was simply incapable of behaving in any other manner. Her grief was real."

So, too, with Theresa. Years after Clara's death, when Theresa set out to purloin Louis's money, she hadn't been out to cheat her friend's daughter; she was simply incapable of behaving otherwise. She had cared for Clara, but in her world—that maelstrom of Corleone siblings—if you wanted something, you had to try to get it; otherwise, someone else would. It was this code that gave her the balls to do whatever had to be done, legal or not, for my mother.

Theresa's behavior wouldn't have surprised my mother, because she came from a family that lived by the same code. She was one of them—or maybe she wasn't tough enough to be one of them without getting depressed.

My mother didn't tell my father she had diabetes because you didn't tell anything if you didn't have to. That wasn't betrayal; it was the way things were. Afterwards, well, she thought the marriage would work out. She never expected his family to keep on remembering. As time went on, she turned more and more to her look-alike sibling Bernie, her think-alike friend Theresa. As in that long-ago movie, I see the face of Joan Crawford—

Theresa changing until the face resembles my mother's.

Accepting the new look gives me indigestion, but at the same time, I can't resist reaching for another helping of Janet's fabulous chopped liver.

"My mother never cooked, you know," Janet says, "except for some kind of Italian potato pancake with cheese in it."

I remember that my mother didn't cook much either, except for an occasional pancake, no cheese, on Sunday morning.

Okay, some kind of sisters, I'll admit. Pass the Pepto-Bismol.

10

A Woman In Pieces

JANET IS A COLORFUL storyteller. She tells me that, when Theresa was in the hospital, dying, Hurricane Andrew hit Miami, aiming straight for Theresa's house. The city was in chaos— rivers of water, entire streets impassable. Theresa wasn't aware of much, but she heard the news reports, and she begged Janet to save her possessions.

Janet donned rain gear and hip boots and, toting a baseball bat to ward off looters, hastened to the house, only to find the area cordoned off by police. Somehow she pushed her way through, and while the police were distracted, gained entry to the house. Inside, the water was knee-deep, mildew beginning to sprout on furniture.

Sloshing her way to the bedroom, Janet opened the clothes closet, and there, amid a sea of ruination, floated the fragments of the bust my mother had sculpted of Minnie, the bust that had once stood on the credenza in our living room, the bust we were always so careful not to break—shattered.

After my mother died, Janet says, Theresa took the bust (how did you miss that one, Bronx Surrogate's Court?) and kept it with her always. When she married Mr. Konigsberg, and then Mr. Levinson, wherever she set up her gypsy camp, the bust was prominent. In Ann Landers' column, I've read letters from second spouses complaining that photos of the first spouse are still around. But Theresa's case is even more extreme. *Dear Ann, I know my wife loves me, but she insists on having a bust of her former mother-in-law in our bedroom. Have you ever heard of anything like this? Am I being too sensitive, Ann?* Well, yes, you are, buddy, if you want Theresa—and plenty of men seem to have wanted her.

I don't know how much Theresa cared for those men, but this bust-schlepping is evidence of a genuine attachment to Minnie—and to my mother, the work's creator.

"If the bust had been in one piece, I would have given it to you," Janet says. I believe her. She seems to have a generous spirit.

Later, flying home to New Jersey, I think about the bust. A darkened airplane is the perfect place for reflection, if one isn't watching the movie. Flickering images—

images one can ignore—liberate the mind. How ironic, I think, that my search, which began with Minnie's death certificate, ends with Minnie—in pieces, a perfect metaphor, because here, at the end, after plotting, digging, imagining, and driving a great many people mad, all I've found of my mother is bits and pieces. And that is all I am going to get.

Was it worthwhile to dive into the "mess," retrieving whatever pieces I could discover or invent? Worthwhile to be seduced by old gossip, get mired in the lousy year 1946? Yes. After sloshing through the mud, I feel more complete, more of a piece myself. Before my search, I was like "little half-chick" in the fairy tale. I had half a family, and I had to hop along, unsteady on my feet. Now I've got enough pieces of the other half to keep me balanced.

A search ends when the searcher becomes sated. A search ends when the person she finds is herself.

I imagine that I'm in Janet's boots in 1992 when Hurricane Andrew strikes. I sashay past the police, push open Theresa's front door, and stand in the sopping wet carpet. My boots squeak as I pass a damask sofa covered in plastic, gilt-edged mirrors, a pedestal table, and an endless array of *tchotchkes*—statuettes of animals, ballet dancers, Hummel children, maybe even a saint or two now that she's returned to her roots, outlived the Jewish husbands.

In the closet, I think I see those sequined gowns of yesteryear, the platform shoes I so admired. Get real. Theresa would have been too old to trot about in platforms, yet I can't imagine her in senior citizen jogging suits, pants with elasticized waists, canvas shoes that close with Velcro. Never that, never.

Looking down, I spot the fragments of floating statuary beckoning like votive candles. I kneel, gaze into the water, and the pieces come together; the shape they take isn't Minnie's but my own. I don't share a single facial feature with Minnie, yet I've become the bust my mother sculpted, the legacy she left.

I see what becomes of a child whose mother can only be understood in pieces. I understand that the child grows into a woman, forever seeking, doubting herself—a streak of insecurity a mile deep that begins with her mother's absences and, particularly, her strange final absence. I understand that my lifelong quest for security, the peaceful feeling in Solomon's arms, arises out of the "mess." My father was with me after death because I know him; I was raised by his surrogates. She was the ephemeral, undiscovered source of my being. Not knowing her made me fragile. Not knowing her made me fear I might wind up like her. If only I could have saved her, I might have saved myself.

In this book, I have tried to do just that. I have made myself attendant to my mother's Humpty Dumpty falls, and I even invented the falls myself, so that, at last, I could put her together again. All the Kings' Horses and All the King's Men can't do the job, but the queen's daughter—the Queen of Bohemia's daughter—*she* can.

The daughter of a woman in pieces is always picking up pieces, sometimes in anger, sometimes in love. She becomes a super-nurturer, responsible for everything, looking out for victims, doing repair work. She serves on the board of battered women's shelters, she volunteers at homeless shelters, she leads the charge when a local teacher gets accused falsely, the daughter believes, of child abuse.

And she wants so little for herself. If they had to depend on her, the shopping networks would go out of business. "Don't you ever want anything, Mom?" her daughter declares in frustration as they stroll through a department store. Why are you always buying things for other people—why, why, why?

Because there are so many pieces to be picked up. Because my mother passed on to me her social-conscience gene, along with a breast-cancer gene. She made me a community volunteer, an organizer of worthwhile projects, a political activist. She made me intensely caring in the Teacher's Union way, about the world of issues, the only world that counts.

Another thing: I'm lovable, so they must have been doing something right, the Sonkins, and sometime before them, before she disappeared, she must have been doing something right, too. She was the Little Engine that Almost Could—a few more chugs, a little more help from Dr. Wallace, or perhaps a little less—and she could have been over the mountain. She could have been a feisty old woman like Emily and Anna. She could have been in an assisted-living facility like Aunt Sylvia, visited weekly by me, worried about daily by me, "the responsible party" to use the institution's phrase.

I'm the "responsible party" who sought out her pieces, dreamed up her pieces, and now I'm going to take them home, and put them on a shelf, next to Sarah Zishe's candlesticks. And if a hurricane doesn't wreck my peaceful little town, they will be there for years to come.

Solomon asks, "Are you finished with all this now?" Never finished but more content, I tell him. Thank you for loving me.

The candlesticks are happy. They have family company, at last, the gene gang together. "Biddie-bum, biddie-bum," they sing. "Biddie-bye, biddie-bye." They look at the sun streaming through our wall of windows. Light, light, everywhere. Who could ask for anything more?

Grandma Minnie and Grandpa Louis, mid-1930s

The Sonkin family, mid-1920s. Left to right, front row, Uncle Robert and Aunt Sylvia; back row, my father Daniel, Grandma Katie, and Grandpa Philip.

My mother Clara, far right, back row, in the Catskills, 1920s

My mother and me, 1937

My mother and father and me

Grandpa Louis and me, 1937

At Camp Meadowbrook in the Berkshires, 1941. I am sitting on the counselor's lap.

With Aunt Sylvia, 1948

With Uncle Robert and Aunt Sylvia, 1948

BUREAU OF RECORDS
Filed DEPARTMENT OF HEALTH
BOROUGH OF MANHATTAN

1940 MAR 9 PM 9 03

Certificate of Death

Certificate No. 2505

1. NAME OF DECEASED (Print) MINNIE (First Name) (Middle Name) PALEY (Last Name)

PERSONAL AND STATISTICAL PARTICULARS (May be filled in by Funeral Director)

2 USUAL RESIDENCE: (If non-resident, give place and state) Borough Bronx
No. 1520 Sheridan Ave.

3 SINGLE, MARRIED, WIDOWED, OR DIVORCED (write the word) Married

4 WIFE of Louis Paley

5 DATE OF BIRTH OF DECEDENT (Month) March (Day) 15 (Year) 1880

6 AGE 59 yrs. — mos. das. If LESS than 1 day, hrs. or min.

7 OCCUPATION
A Trade, profession, or particular kind of work, as planer, sawyer, bookkeeper, etc. Housewife
B Industry or business in which work was done, as silk mill, sawmill, bank, etc. —
C Date deceased last worked at this occupation (month and year) 1937
D Total time (years) spent in this occupation 35 yrs.

8 BIRTHPLACE (State or country) Russia

9 How long in U. S. (if of foreign birth) 48 yrs.
10 How long resident in City of New York 48 yrs.

PARENTS OF DECEASED
11 NAME OF FATHER OF DECEDENT Sholem Podnus
12 BIRTHPLACE OF FATHER (State or country) Russia
13 MAIDEN NAME OF MOTHER OF DECEDENT Sarah Kupchnikel
14 BIRTHPLACE OF MOTHER (State or country) Russia

15 SIGNATURE OF INFORMANT Irving I Paley
RELATIONSHIP TO DECEASED Son
ADDRESS 2765 Kingsbridge Terr.

MEDICAL CERTIFICATE OF DEATH (To be filled in by the physician)

16 PLACE OF DEATH: Borough Bronx
No. 1520 Sheridan Ave.
(If in hospital or other institution, give name instead of street and number)

17 DATE AND HOUR OF DEATH (Month) March (Day) 9 (Year) 1940 (Hour) 3:55 P.M.

18 SEX Female
19 COLOR OR RACE White
20 APPROXIMATE AGE 59 yrs.

21 I HEREBY CERTIFY that I attended the deceased from Jan. 1937 to March 9 1940, that I last saw her alive on March 9 1940, and that the facts stated in items 16-20 are correct.

I further certify that death did NOT occur as the result of accident, homicide, suicide, criminal abortion, acute or chronic poisoning, or in any suspicious or unusual manner.

Statement of cause of death is based on autopsy; operation; laboratory test; clinical findings only. (Cross out terms that do not apply.)

Principal cause of death	Date of Onset
Carcinoma of the Breast	Oct 1939
Carcinoma of the Rectum	March 1937
Contributory causes and other conditions: Metastasis to liver, lungs	Jan 1940

Autopsy: Date of (If none, so state)
Operation: Date of (If none, so state)
Condition for which performed
Dates of laboratory tests

Signature Jacob Eiben [illegible] M. D.
Address 1883 Prospect Ave NYC

24 PLACE OF BURIAL OR CREMATION Mt Lebanon Cemetery
DATE OF BURIAL OR CREMATION March 10 1940

25 FUNERAL DIRECTOR Kaslan Sons Inc
ADDRESS 4515 Ft Ham P Kway
PERMIT NUMBER 2016

BUREAU OF RECORDS 2016 DEPARTMENT OF HEALTH CITY OF NEW YORK

Minnie Paley's death certificate, March 1940

BOARD OF EDUCATION OF THE CITY OF NEW YORK
HAROLD O. LEVY, *Chancellor*

OFFICE OF THE CHANCELLOR
110 LIVINGSTON STREET - BROOKLYN, NY 11201

DIVISION OF FINANCIAL OPERATIONS
BUREAU OF EMPLOYEE SUPPORT SERVICES
OFFICE OF EMPLOYMENT RECORDS RESEARCH
49 Flatbush Ave. Ext. - 8th Floor, Brooklyn, NY 11201

Name: Jean Arsleiter
Address: 329 Park Ave
Leonia, N.J. 07605
Attn:
To:

CASE EXAMINER: M Lewter
Date: MAR 7 - 2000
Referral Number: 29
Re: Paley, Clara (Sorkin)
File #: 41164 SS #: —

The Office of Employment Records Research records indicate that Ms. Paley ~~served as a~~ hasn't served in the New York City School System during the following period(s):

PERIOD	MONTHS	DAYS	SESSIONS	HOURS	MIN	RATE	GROSS	TITLE	LOCATION
9/29-6/45	Records Unavailable								
45/46	No Service Indicated								
46/47		"			"				

Frederick J. Thomsen, Manager
Office of Employment Records Research

Record request response from the City of New York Board of Education, March 2000

www.ingramcontent.com/pod-product-compliance
Lightning Source LLC
Chambersburg PA
CBHW022119080426
42734CB00006B/181

* 9 7 8 1 9 3 8 8 1 2 0 8 8 *